IMAGES OF **150 YEARS** OF THE

METROPOLITAN RAILWAY

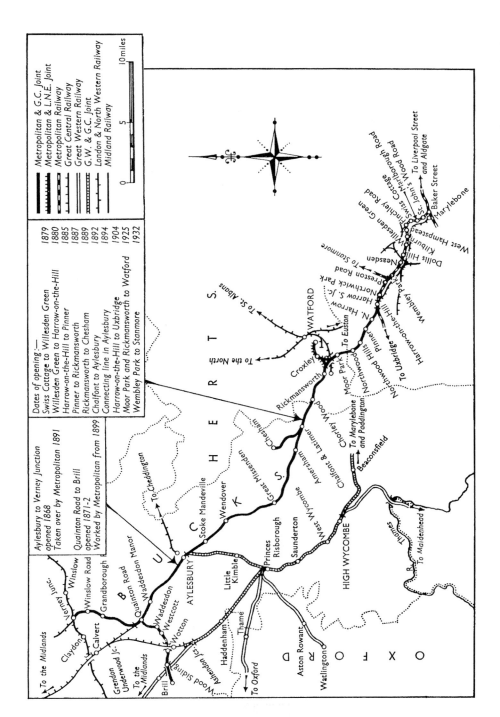

Map showing the Metropolitan Railway and its Joint companies in relation to other railways. (The Railway Magazine)

Legend:

Metropolitan & G.C. Joint	
Metropolitan & L.N.E. Joint	
Metropolitan Railway	
Great Central Railway	
Great Western Railway	
G.W. & G.C. Joint	
London & North Western Railway	
Midland Railway	

Dates of opening:—

Swiss Cottage to Willesden Green	1879
Willesden Green to Harrow-on-the-Hill	1880
Harrow-on-the-Hill to Pinner	1885
Pinner to Rickmansworth	1887
Rickmansworth to Chesham	1889
Chalfont to Aylesbury	1892
Connecting line in Aylesbury	1894
Harrow-on-the-Hill to Uxbridge	1904
Moor Park and Rickmansworth to Watford	1925
Wembley Park to Stanmore	1932

Aylesbury to Verney Junction opened 1868
Taken over by Metropolitan 1891

Quainton Road to Brill opened 1871-2
Worked by Metropolitan from 1899

10 miles
0   5

IMAGES OF **150 YEARS** OF THE

METROPOLITAN RAILWAY

DR CLIVE FOXELL CBE FRENG

I know a land where the wild flowers grow,
Near, near at hand if by train you go,
Metro-land, Metro-land,
Meadows sweet have a golden glow,
Hills are green as the vales below,
In Metro-land, Metro-land.

George Robert Sims (1847–1922)
– possibly the first mention of 'Metroland'

The History Press

ACKNOWLEDGEMENTS

Relevant illustrations are vital to a book of this kind and therefore I have tried to include ones which will be fresh to many of the readers. However, there are few photographs available that were taken in the early period of this story and those of important events tend to be familiar, but I have included some of these to provide a comprehensive survey. I am therefore most grateful to all those who have provided photographs and I have tried to credit these where possible. Nevertheless, in the case of 'orphan works' where origin/owner/copyright is confused or unknown, I have performed the suggested diligent searches and apologise for any incorrect attributions.

No book about the Met would be possible without drawing on the resources of London Transport Museum and I am very grateful for the assistance of Simon Murphy, curator of their photo archive. The Brent Archive has also been helpful and I would like to thank past photographers: John Parnham, Robert Clark, C.R.L. Coles, Stephen Gradidge, Ron Potter and H.C. Casserley. Also David Bosher for use of the Fred Ivey Collection, Les Reason, Ron White and the many others mentioned in the captions. Such captions are also an important element and I wish to thank Richard Hardy for his sage advice, Len Bunning and Desmond Croome for reviewing these for errors and also my daughter, Elizabeth Foxell, for proofreading the draft; any remaining errors are my own responsibility.

Front cover illustration: The K Class 2-6-4T locomotives were the most powerful of the Met fleet. Here No.116 is breasting the highest point on the line, over the Chilterns at Dutchlands, with a train for Aylesbury in 1935. *(NRM/Science & Society Picture Library)*. *Back cover*: The original concept of the new sub-surface stock, of which an eight-car variant is replacing all the existing Metropolitan Line stock. *(Bombardier)*

First published 2012

The History Press
The Mill, Brimscombe Port
Stroud, Gloucestershire, GL5 2QG
www.thehistorypress.co.uk

British Library Cataloguing in Publication Data.
A catalogue record for this book is available from the British Library.

ISBN 978 0 7524 7009 2

Typesetting and origination by The History Press
Printed in Great Britain
Manufacturing managed by Jellyfish Print Solutions Ltd

CONTENTS

INTRODUCTION

Some may question why the 150th anniversary of the Metropolitan Railway, being one of the smaller railways in this country, deserves to be celebrated. However, the 'Met' has had a surprisingly significant role in the evolution of our railways and has retained some of its idiosyncratic ways through many traumas. So the author felt it was appropriate to mark the event by publishing a collection of photographs to try to capture the charm and variety of the Met that has been embedded in the memories of the millions who have travelled on the line or lived in that area, evocatively called 'Metroland'.

By the 1830s the City of London solicitor, Charles Pearson, had become concerned about the inadequate state of its infrastructure under the pressure of an increasing population of workers who had to live in London. This resulted in 300,000 horses drawing traffic sharing the roads with 2.5 million other animals each year herded to the city abattoirs. However, Pearson realised that this horrendous congestion was about to be made worse by the construction of the new mainline railway termini on the margins of the city. Pearson now sought to ease congestion by means of an underground railway along the periphery of the city. Inevitably there were delays in implementing his scheme due to funding, Parliament and economic vagaries, but the major public concern was over travelling underground, in the dark, hauled by a fiery engine. However, this fear was alleviated by the construction of long railway tunnels such as that at Woodhead in 1845. Eventually a respected businessman, William Mallins, proposed a line to run under the New Road linking the railway termini and, after difficulty raising the capital, an input from the Great Western Railway (to assure access for their trains) allowed work to start.

The senior engineer was Sir John Fowler, but the vital tunnelling was undertaken by Benjamin Baker using the 'cut and cover' method and although many difficulties were encountered, the line of some 3 miles and 65 chains from Paddington to Farringdon was completed in January 1863. However, the special locomotive designed by Fowler to avoid smoke emission was a failure and the first train on 10 January was hauled by a modified GWR engine. But due to disagreement over access, the GWR withdrew their stock and the Met had to turn to Beyer-Peacock to supply some of their engines intended for export to fill the gap. In spite of this, the Met was a great success with almost 10 million passengers being carried in the first year, which led to the line being extended to Moorgate, South Kensington and Hammersmith by 1868. Indeed, all seemed well with profits of 7 per cent, but it was discovered that the chairman had achieved this by dubious accounting and he was replaced by an apparently reputable railwayman, Edward Watkin.

Watkin came from a Manchester textile family but started his career by becoming secretary to a minor railway company which happened to become a vital piece in the 'jigsaw puzzle' that was the Railway Mania. This experience shaped his complex character: ruthless with enemies, charismatic with shareholders, 'hands on' with his companies, using politics and the media – and very secretive with all. He became an MP and confidant of Gladstone and involved in many companies here and abroad. In spite of having many 'irons in the fire' he managed the Met firmly but employed some dubious financial practices to achieve his personal objectives. For little did they know, that in the context of his obsession with international trade, he wished to link Paris and Manchester by rail – and the Met would be part of it!

Without revealing his plan, he gradually extended the Met to the north-west towards his Manchester, Sheffield & Lincolnshire Railway (MS&LR) whilst to the south he was able to join his South Eastern Railway to Folkestone. He then started work on the first Channel Tunnel to link with his Chemin de Fer du Nord to reach Paris. So the Met was driven from Baker Street into the countryside at Finchley Road and then on the surface to meet the primitive Aylesbury & Buckingham Railway (A&BR), which Watkin soon brought up to mainline standards whilst extending his MS&LR southwards to join it. But the respective managers of the Met and the MS&LR, realising that a merger seemed inevitable, resorted to delaying tactics. The pressures on Watkin were now increasing with additional problems from his Channel Tunnel and a controversial new London terminal. As a result he suffered a series of strokes which gradually affected his ability to control his projects and although he witnessed the opening of his new Marylebone station in 1899, he died soon afterwards and his empire disintegrated.

So the new line from the north (renamed the Great Central), based on sharing tracks with the Met into London, created an uneasy relationship which contributed to a major disaster in 1904. With both railways under new management, it was realised that they had to collaborate and a Joint Committee was established to manage the shared line. However, as the two companies had different objectives, with new projects and sharing revenues remaining matters of contention, the Joint arrangement had a major influence on the evolution of the Met. Even with various changes of ownership this Joint arrangement continued until 1948 and forms the basis of current operations.

The Met was left with a strong business based on the Inner Circle, but the extension into rural Buckinghamshire was a liability. However, the new manager, Robert Selbie, found that many of Watkin's follies could be turned into advantages by creating what he called Metroland as a desirable housing development which would generate a new commuter market. To sustain this traffic, Selbie introduced modern rolling stock, more electrification and the services of a mainline railway. The success of the iconic Metroland campaign made the Met the most profitable of the London suburban railways, but the London deep-tube lines, under the banner of the *UndergrounD*, supported the government's desire to amalgamate all forms of London's transport. Reluctantly, in 1933 the Met was forced into the new London Transport (LT).

Under Frank Pick, LT naturally wished to standardise all its activities and this meant the loss of many of the Met's idiosyncratic ways, but the extra clout of LT resulted in funding to improve many of the Met's bottlenecks and electrify the route to Amersham. The latter was delayed by the Second World War, during which the Met suffered badly from the Blitz, and deferred maintenance was to have a lasting effect on reliability. The post-war period has been characterised by the inability of governments to deal with the inherent problem of loss-making railways. Nationalisation in 1948 resulted in an ever-changing organisation and policies typified by Marylebone almost being closed. This was succeeded in 1998 by a pseudo privatisation of which the greatest success has been the creation of Chiltern Railways, which has revitalised Marylebone services and collaborated in sharing the Met route. LT was eventually put under the wing of the Greater London Council. Nevertheless, after the war LT was able to restart the electrification project, completing it in 1961 with new A60 multiple-electric stock.

But the future role of the Met has often been in doubt due to financial, political and other pressures. At one time it was even proposed that Cross Rail would replace some services and briefly it was transferred into a Private Finance Initiative under Metronet before returning to the LT fold in Transport *for* London. In spite of these traumas the Met now has new trains – the S stock – which should carry it on into its 200th year.

ONE

CHARLES PEARSON
FATHER OF THE UNDERGROUND RAILWAY

Charles Pearson (1793–1862). The solicitor of the City of London became concerned with the lack of infrastructure as the town grew and proposed an underground railway to ease congestion. Although he did not live to see the opening of the railway, his widow was given a pension to mark his efforts. *(Unknown origin)*

◀ This picture of London Bridge shows the extent of the congestion in the mid-nineteenth century due to the growth of the population and its reliance on horse-drawn transport of over 300,000 animals. Indeed, this was made worse by the 2.5 million cattle that were herded each year from the Home Counties into the city for slaughter to feed the people. *(Clive Foxell Coll.)*

▶ At the time when Pearson proposed an underground railway to ease the congestion in London, many people still regarded steam railways with horror, as illustrated by this contemporary cartoon. It shows a locomotive monster descending on a family in its path screaming, 'I come to eat you'. Added to this was the fear of travelling underground in total darkness, which increased opposition to Pearson's scheme. *(Illustrated London News (ILN))*

▲ By the time work actually started on the Metropolitan Railway in 1861, such fears had been assuaged to some extent. During this period many grandiose schemes were found to be impracticable and the accepted solution was based on the 'cut and cover' technique where a large trench was dug down the relevant roads, a brick tunnel built just below the surface and the road restored. This shows the construction of Baker Street station. (ILN)

▼ Nevertheless, the problem of smoke and steam from the engines filling the tunnels remained. So the chief engineer, the eminent Sir John Fowler, devised a fireless locomotive in which the boiler was heated by hot bricks inserted in its firebox at every station, and the picture shows the engine on one of its trials. Regrettably it did not work. But note the broad-gauge rail added to the Met standard gauge at the insistence of the GWR. (ILN)

▲ Fortunately the GWR was prepared to assist by building some special 2-4-0 well-tank engines, modified so that their exhaust was condensed by feeding it into the cold-water tanks. This painting by C. Hamilton–Ellis shows one such locomotive, *Wasp*, at Baker Street station during the opening of the Met in 1863. In the foreground are Sir John Fowler, Sir Benjamin Baker (responsible for the tunnelling) and their wives. *(London Transport Museum (LTM))*

▼ In contrast to the underground stations, wherever possible surface stations such as Aldgate were built in a way that would reduce the remaining problems with smoke. Whilst some doctors recommended travelling on the smoke-filled Met to cure chest problems, enterprising chemists near the station entrances at road level offered 'Met' cough mixtures to ease the suffering of the passengers. *(ILN)*

▲ Lack of their own engines was an embarrassment to the Met, compounded by an acrimonious relationship with the GWR. So they sought a possible 'ready made' supplier and found that Beyer-Peacock had developed an engine for the Tudela & Bilbao Railway which could be modified with suitable condensing apparatus. The above-mentioned A Class 4-4-0T engines were extremely successful and were the mainstay of Met services for many years. *(R.P. Hendry)*

▼ With the completion of the Inner Circle, the A Class, and later B Class variants, were providing an intensive ten-minute interval service and the Met workshops had an uphill struggle to maintain them. Here is an A Class engine in the workshops stripped for repairs. As the Met expanded they took on even more duties, but their reign ended with the electrification of the Inner Circle on 24 September 1905. *(R.P. Hendry)*

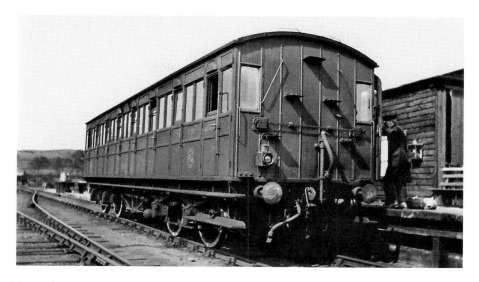

▲ The early four- and eight-wheeled coaches were notorious 'boneshakers' and this shows one of these rigid eight-wheeled types at the end of its life, having been relegated to the Brill branch. The first-class compartments were relatively luxurious with upholstered seats, curtains and carpets, compared to the second class with seats covered with oilcloth and the third class with benches and bare woodwork. *(R.P. Hendry)*

▼ A close-up of one of the rigid axle boxes of the early eight-wheeled coach. This one was built by Brown-Marshall and others by Oldbury and by Ashbury, incorporating various methods of allowing some lateral movement of the axles to reduce damage to the flanges of the wheels. Initially, the Met trains relied on the engine for braking but this coach later had vacuum brakes fitted. *(R.P. Hendry)*

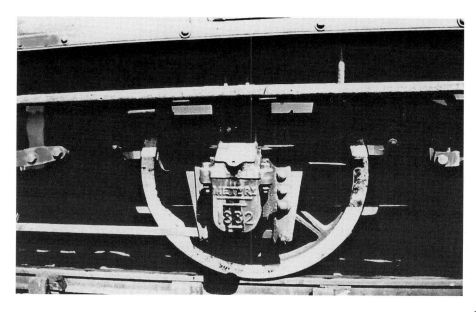

TWO

EDWARD WATKIN TAKES OVER

Although the Met was very successful, by 1872 serious accounting problems emerged and a new chairman was appointed – Edward Watkin. He was already experienced in railway affairs but had his own agenda, which was to use the Met to help create a major new railway. *(C.A.F. Coll.)*

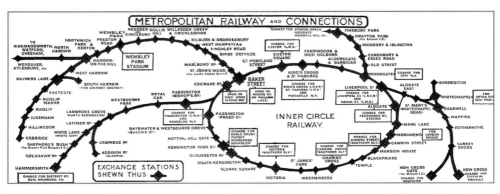

▲ Initially, Watkin had to rely on the existing A/B Class locomotives as he began to extend the Met. However, they were capable of the onerous new tasks involving heavier loads and gradients. Here a group of Met staff cluster around an A Class tank engine at Baker Street station. No.9 was originally named *Minerva* and has been given a new stovepipe chimney and larger coal bunker. *(C.A.F. Coll.)*

▼ Because the existing engine sheds and works at Edgware Road were overcrowded, Watkin decided to build a new facility at Neasden on the route he intended to use to the north. This was then in open countryside and he had to add housing for the Met staff. This shows a group of them having attended a meeting in nearby Gladstone Park. *(C.A.F. Coll.)*

▲ John Fowler persuaded the Met to form a joint company with the GWR to extend the line to Hammersmith, opening in 1864. The venture proved to be a source of ongoing acrimony with the GWR which Watkin inherited, but he saw it as another way of extending southwards. This picture of A Class engines at Hammersmith was taken before the broad-gauge rails were removed in 1869. *(C.A.F. Coll.)*

▼ In 1869 the new East London Railway opened a railway beneath the River Thames between Wapping (shown below) and Rotherhithe through the earlier pedestrian Brunel Tunnel. It soon got into financial difficulties and after Watkin had been appointed receiver he became chairman and developed the railway as a link between his Met and South Eastern Railways at New Cross, which allowed his trains to run to Folkestone. *(ILN)*

▶ John Fowler was also behind the St John's Wood Railway of 1864, a single-track spur from Baker Street which petered out at Swiss Cottage. The above picture shows the construction looking south towards the main station. Again, this was inherited by Watkin who used it to launch his major extension of the Met towards his northern railways. *(ILN)*

▶ By 1879 Watkin had upgraded the St John's Wood Line to mainline standards and then through open countryside reached Neasden in 1880. Later on, this picture shows the scene at Neasden & Kingsbury station with a Harrow-bound train headed by a stalwart A Class tank engine passing a C Class No.67 for Baker Street with a rake of the rough-riding Oldbury rigid eight-wheeler coaches. *(S. Gradidge Coll.)*

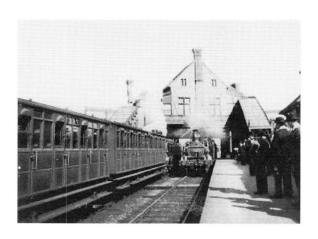

▶ One of the first Met engines, a condensing A Class 4–4–0T No.2 was built in 1864 and initially carried the name *Mars*. Delivered by Beyer-Peacock some sixteen years before the Met extension reached Harrow, here it is seen running light near the temporary bridge that was to become Station Road. The engine is still without a proper cab for conditions outside the Inner Circle and was scrapped in 1907. *(J.E. Connor LRR)*

▲ Until the Met extension was built through Middlesex and Buckinghamshire, the local people had to rely on coach services to take them to the London North Western Line from Euston. Here is such a horse-drawn coach waiting at Pinner, outside the fire station and Red Lion public house, to take passengers to Watford station. The bus had a rear entrance, with luggage on the roof. *(C.A.F. Coll.)*

▼ This picture is believed to be of the first train at Pinner on 25 May 1885. The staff pose around a highly polished A Class Met engine with its train of the rough-riding four-wheeler coaches. Rickmansworth was reached in 1887 and then Watkin had to decide whether to proceed north via High Wycombe, Amersham or Chesham. *(LTM)*

▲ The line to Chesham went via Chalfont Road, then as a single track down the Chess Valley to a station in the town, paid for by the locals. The inspection of the line on 15 May 1889 was a major event, as seen above, when the whole populace celebrated as a Firbank's contractor's train arrived with Watkin and others for a grand banquet in the Goods Shed. *(Ray East Coll.)*

▼ The first public train left Chesham on 8 July with more muted celebrations, but for a wager two young men travelled to France and back within the day! The engine was an A Class tank No.4, originally named *Mercury* and built in 1864, and the leading coach has the curved tops to its doors to allow opening within the Inner Circle tunnels. A turntable had been built to avoid running with the cab first. *(Ray East Coll.)*

⏶ Here at the controls of an early A/B Class 4-4-0T locomotive the stoic Met driver has no cab in order to give more ventilation in the original underground section of the Met, where the choking fumes were a hazard. However, on the surface section along the extension there was no protection from the elements. The high parts over the Chilterns even had fences to reduce snowdrifts. *(Getty Images)*

⏷ From 1895 most of the A Class engines were fitted with cabs to give some protection for the crews. Here one such, No.46, is shown at Hodd's Wood, near Chesham Bois on the Chesham Line where it was derailed due to a broken coupling rod. This was probably caused by the stress generated by the frequent braking and starting at the numerous stations on the Inner Circle. *(Ray East Coll.)*

▲ As his hope for extending the Chesham Line to Tring failed, Watkin drove the Met on from Chalfont Road towards Aylesbury. This was the traditional ceremony in 1891 to mark the start of work by 'turning the first turf', at Stoke Road about half a mile south of Aylesbury. This would join the existing Aylesbury & Buckingham Railway (A&BR) station in 1892. *(C.A.F. Coll.)*

▼ The A&BR was a light railway running north to Buckingham, built by friends of Watkin – Sir Harry Verney and the Duke of Buckingham. Watkin took over this primitive line and upgraded it to take the Met north to Verney Junction. This is an early picture of Aylesbury station, shared with the GWR who used the platform on the left, whilst the A&BR trains used the right-hand one. *(S. G. Payne)*

▲ This 1868 picture of Winslow Road station on the A&BR in the middle of the rural Vale of Aylesbury shows the very basic single-line construction, with light flat-bottomed rails nailed to the sleepers. Perhaps the young station man was the original Winslow Boy? Watkin soon built a standard Met station. *(LTM)*

▼ In acquiring the A&BR, Watkin also became responsible for the Brill Tramway which had been built privately by the Duke of Buckingham to serve his estate. It also interested Watkin because there were plans to extend to Oxford. This scene of about 1900 shows Watkin's upgraded line at Quainton Road with the Brill branch train in the bay on the right. *(C.A.F. Coll.)*

▲ As Watkin extended the Met to the north, he became conscious that the stalwart A/B Class engines needed to be replaced by more powerful types. Bearing in mind the limited facilities at Neasden, he arranged for another of his companies, the SER, to supply four of their Q Class 0-4-4T engines, to be known as the Met C Class. *(C.A.F. Coll.)*

▼ Initially some light LNWR engines had been hired to work the Met trains beyond Aylesbury but in 1894 the company bought some six 2-4-0T locomotives from Sharp, Stewart & Co. (modified for their needs). However, these D Class engines do not seem to have been successful and were soon relegated to other duties, all being sold by 1923. *(R.C. Riley)*

▲ In the light of favourable experience with the C Class, T.F. Clarke designed a larger version of the 0-4-4T and the first two were built at Neasden, being classified as E Class. In 1900 four more were supplied by Hawthorn, Leslie & Co. and these classic passenger locomotives took on the most onerous duties, including hauling a Royal Train from Baker Street to Amersham in 1908. *(R.P. Hendry)*

▼ One of the elegant Met E Class 0-4-4T engines, with their brightly polished brass domes, in action near Chorleywood. The down train is bound for the Chesham branch. They proved worthy successors to the valiant A Class engines and later continued to provide standby duties at Rickmansworth and Aylesbury until the 1950s. *(Colin Seabright)*

▲ In 1897 the Met bought two 0-6-0 Peckett saddle tank engines mainly for shunting duties at Harrow and Neasden. One of their duties was handling the large volume of coal for Neasden Power Station. Under the terms of the later Met & GC Joint operation, such shunting on their line had to be shared, so the Peckett tanks were often in storage. *(H.C. Casserley)*

▼ Responding to the growth of goods traffic, the Met bought 0-6-2T F Class engines from the Yorkshire Engine Co. in 1901, to a Clark design based on his E Class with a different wheel arrangement. They were the last type that could enter the Met/Inner Circle south of Finchley Road and be in the original Met style. They were the mainstay of goods motive power until Robert Selbie's engines appeared. *(R.P. Hendry)*

▲ Watkin was a fervent Francophile and in 1890 this led him to acquire 280 acres of land at Wembley for pleasure gardens to feature a rival to the Eiffel Tower. Although under the auspices of a separate company, in practice it was subsidised by the Met. With Sir Benjamin Baker as engineer, by 1894 the tower had risen to the first stage and appeared in Met publicity. (*H. Lascelles*)

▼ A rare view from the platform at the first stage of Watkin's Tower showing the extent of the pleasure gardens which initially attracted a large number of visitors. In the distance is Wembley Park station from which a branch line had been laid to bring materials for constructing the tower. This line was also used by Watkin for experiments with electrification. (*Brent Archive*)

▶ Meanwhile, Watkin had been gradually extending his MS&LR south from Nottingham to join with the Met at Quainton Road. In parallel, he was building a magnificent new London terminus for the line at Marylebone. The top picture shows his new line being built where it leaves the Met at West Hampstead and diverges at Canfield Place into a tunnel emerging at Marylebone. The middle scene shows the most controversial part of the tunnel which passed under the hallowed turf of Lords. The bottom picture captures the moment when the first train of the new Great Central Railway left Marylebone on 9 March 1899. *(GCRS, LTM, C.A.F. Coll.)*

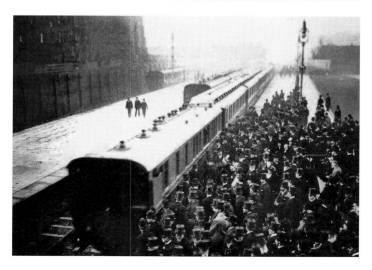

▲ Now the GCR shared the Met between Quainton Road and West Hampstead, as shown here with GCR No.862 (a Pollitt Class 11) on the first up train. The GCR was now running a series of major express and freight trains to London which conflicted with the Met suburban services and this arrangement became more difficult when Watkin had to retire due to ill health. *(John Parnham)*

◀ Because of these operational problems, the GCR formed a joint company with the GWR to create a new mainline into London which would reduce dependence on the Met. This 1898 picture shows the new avoiding lines being built in the shadow of Watkin's Tower, soon to be abandoned due to subsidence. *(LTM)*

▶ At the same time that Watkin's GCR and Met were at loggerheads and his Wembley tower had turned into a 'folly', another piece of his Manchester–Paris scheme came to naught. This picture shows his partly finished Channel Tunnel, with the crude workman's inscription 'this tunnel was begun in 1880', which had to be abandoned due to government fears of a French invasion. *(C.A.F. Coll.)*

▼ With the death of Watkin, the relations between the Met and the GCR became ever more acrimonious and this led to operating problems contributing to a serious crash at Aylesbury in 1904, when the GCR engine below derailed and hit another train. This incident coincided with the retirement of the opposing managers and led to a formal agreement on how to share the line. *(R. Sedgewick)*

❖ THREE ❖

THE MET & GC JOINT COMMITTEE

The Joint Committee to run the equally shared railway came into force in 1906; in this all activities were rotated between the companies every five years. Fortunately the new managers – Robert Selbie (Met, left) and Sam Fay (GCR, right) – were more pragmatic than their predecessors. *(C.A.F. Coll.)*

METROPOLITAN & GREAT CENTRAL
— JOINT COMMITTEE Nº 1 —
TO BE RETURNED TO NORTHWOOD

MET & GC JOINT COMMITTEE.
TRESPASSERS WILL BE PROSECUTED.
PENALTY   FORTY SHILLING OR
IMPRISONMENT FOR   ONE MONTH.

METROPOLITAN AND GREAT CENTRAL
JOINT COMMITTEE.

RESERVED

From_____
To_____
Signed_____
Date_____

DIVISION
OF MAINTENANCE
MET RY GC RY

MI
28½

MET. & G.C. JOINT COMMITTEE

METRO-LAND
WHITSUN
EXCURSIONS

Nº 1 · 1947   PRICE TWOPENCE

METROPOLITAN AND GREAT
CENTRAL JOINT LINE
METROPOLITAN LINE

LNER

UNDERGROUND

TIMETABLE
June 16 · 1947 until further notice

METRO. & L·N·E·RAILWAYS
ENTRANCE TO

WATFORD

PASSENGER STATION. GOODS & COAL DEPÔT.
FREQUENT SERVICES TO LONDON AND ALL PARTS.

The Met & GC Joint Line was a separate company employing staff, operating the trains and controlling the finances. This page of their memorabilia shows how their identity was promulgated and maintained when the GCR became part of the London North Eastern Railway in 1923. Of particular interest is the lineside post some 28½ miles from London indicating where the responsibility for track maintenance changed from the Met to the GCR. (C.A.F. Coll.)

▲ The GCR could now run over the Joint shared line from Harrow (South) to Quainton Road but still had to wait while the Met built separate lines for them from West Hampstead to Harrow. This shows a GCR down express near Chorleywood hauled by a Robinson Class 8D 4-4-2 experimental compound locomotive No.258. *(Locomotive Publishing Co.)*

▼ The more luxurious GCR expresses began to attract passengers away from the Met for the longer journeys and they also introduced competitive through trains from Chesham. Shown here, a Robinson Class 9K 4-4-2T is hauling a train of GCR coaches into Chesham station ready for the return trip to Marylebone. *(Ray East Coll.)*

▲ The GCR took over most of the early morning newspaper deliveries and also worked the Aylesbury–Quainton Road–Verney Junction shuttle service. This turn was usually filled by older and lighter locomotives and this picture shows a Sacré Class 12AM 2-4-0T No.449 simmering in Aylesbury station before such a journey around 1910. *(R. Sedgewick Coll.)*

▼ The only item of rolling stock actually owned by the Joint was this 5-ton 'Accident Hand Crane' No.1 built by Cowans Sheldon in 1914. It spent most of its life at Harrow and then Northwood before being saved and restored by the Buckinghamshire Railway Centre (BRC) at Quainton Road, where many other items of Met & GCR interest are preserved. *(BRC)*

▲ An example which illustrates the independent nature of the Joint is this Met & GC Joint Prize Band comprising staff from the company. Here they are giving a concert in Gladstone Park. *(Brent Archive)*

◄ Various Joint memorabilia. The top row shows parcel stamps from the relevant Joint companies and the middle row the uniform buttons. At the bottom are examples of Joint tickets. *(C.A.F Coll.)*

❖ FOUR ❖

THE ROBERT SELBIE RENAISSANCE

Robert Selbie became secretary
to the Met in 1903 and general
manager in 1908. He was to
revitalise the Met with better
trains – such as the Pullman
services from the city to
Chesham and Verney Junction
– and the concept of Metroland
which made the Met profitable.
(C.A.F. Coll.)

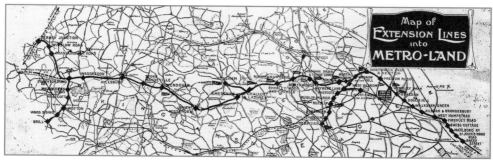

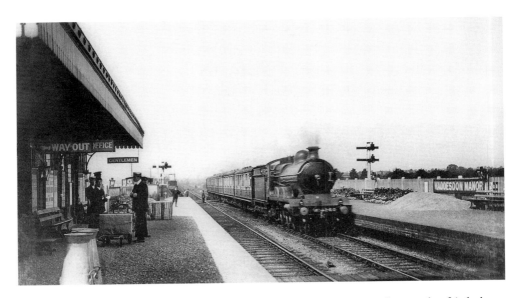

▲ A new station built by the Joint was Waddesdon Manor, some 4 miles north of Aylesbury, to serve the Rothschild Estate more conveniently than the existing one on the Brill branch. Uniquely the buildings were all on the down side. Here a Robinson Atlantic Class 8b No.264 thunders past with an up express to Marylebone. *(J. Smith Coll.)*

▼ The Met upgraded, to some extent, the track and rolling stock of the Brill branch in 1894 but it nevertheless remained something of a backwater. Here, one of the relatively unsuccessful Met D Class light 2-4-0 tank engines has been relegated to duty on the branch and is seen near Waddesdon, later renamed more accurately Waddesdon Road. *(K. Nunn LCGB)*

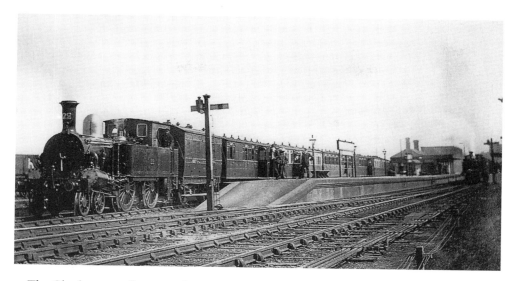

▲ The Chesham travellers complained bitterly about the 'shuttle' service over the branch with its venerable coaches, exposed stations and the time taken for the engine to 'run round' the train at each end of the trip. This scene at Chalfont Road shows Met A Class No.22 (now with cab) with luggage van and rigid eight-wheelers waiting for passengers from the London train. *(Tony Harden Coll.)*

▼ Selbie found that when passengers had a choice of train to travel on the Joint they were increasingly aware of the disparity in quality and comfort between the new GCR services and those of the Met. Here a down Met train headed by an E Class tank is about to pass a GCR Director Class with an express bound for Marylebone. *(P. O'Hind Coll.)*

◄ The previous picture shows that the mainline Met trains were now largely composed of Ashbury bogie carriages, which were at least an improvement over the original rigid four- and eight-wheelers. This picture shows the interior of one of the first-class compartments. The other options were second class or standard, smoking or non-smoking and ladies only. *(Clive Foxell Coll.)*

▲ Selbie was keen to electrify the new branch to Uxbridge, but it had to open with steam traction in July 1904. Here the inaugural train with the Rothschild carriages is pausing at Ruislip headed by a decorated E Class No.1. Along with the Inner Circle, the Met electric services started in 1905, although the link to South Harrow was bedeviled by negotiations with the MDR. *(CAF Coll.)*

▲ Looking east from Edgware Road station on the Inner Circle, around 1905. An A Class tank and train are passing the Met Engine Shed, with a set of multiple-electric stock in a siding. Soon this would be superseded by a larger depot at Neasden. In the background, the new completion from the GCR is manifest by the tower of the recently completed Great Central Hotel. *(C.A.F. Coll.)*

▼ The original Uxbridge station at Belmont Road was built to enable the line to be extended to High Wycombe, but this idea was abandoned. A later scene shows the station being shared by a Piccadilly Line train and a half set of Met electric Ashbury stock, with the motor coach at the rear. *(C.A.F. Coll.)*

▲ To meet the needs of the Met electrification programme, several sets of the steam-hauled Ashbury coaches were converted into electric traction. Unfortunately different types of motor equipment were used so that care had to be taken in forming the sets. Designated M stock, more were converted as the original Ashburys were replaced by the new Dreadnoughts. This shows a set passing the junction for the Watford branch. *(John Parnham)*

▼ The Met now required electric locomotives to haul the longer-distance trains over the newly electrified sections and in 1905 they took delivery of some Westinghouse twin bogie (4 x 200hp) 'camel back' designs. Initially there were many 'teething' problems due to inexperience with this application, but the main difficulty was with the driver's position and his visibility. *(Locomotive Publishing Co.)*

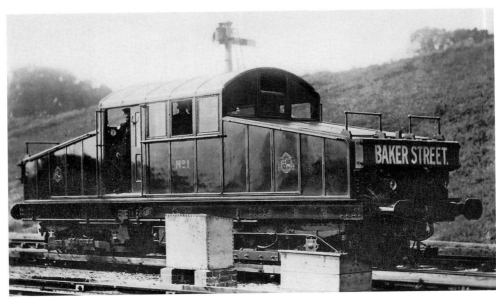

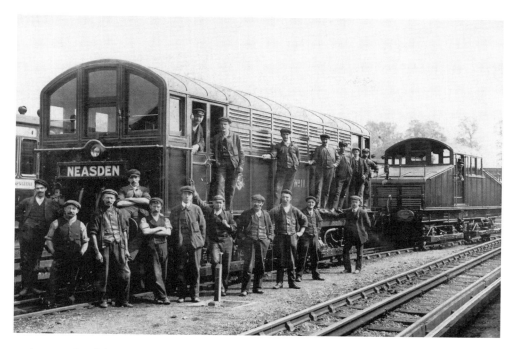

▲ As a result of their poor experience with the 'camel backs' the Met bought an improved design to a more stringent specification from British Thomson-Houston (BT-H) in 1907. Although still of a twin bogie (4 x 215hp) layout, the driver's position was at either end of the locomotive body. This picture taken at Neasden, following delivery of the first locomotive, allows comparison with the previous design. *(Brent Archive)*

▶ An interior view of one of the BT-H locomotives revealing how the electrical control and brake equipment was arranged down the sides of a central gangway, which allowed the driver to move easily from end to end. These machines were quite successful and no major modifications were needed until they were replaced in 1922. *(LTM)*

▲ As part of Selbie's rolling stock improvement programme, a specification was issued in 1919 for electric locomotives to haul the heavier and longer Met trains. For budgetary reasons these were treated as rebuilds of the existing machines, but as can be seen from this picture, many of the new design were being built at Metropolitan-Vickers at the same time. In reality they were new builds. *(LTM)*

▼ The Met proudly showed a 'cut-away' No.15 of the new MV (4 x 300hp) machines at the 1924 British Empire Exhibition and thereafter its driver took the initiative of wearing a 'borrowed' Pullman attendant's white jacket to match the white interior of No.15. Later they were all named and became the classic flagships of the new Met electrified services. *(C.A.F. Coll.)*

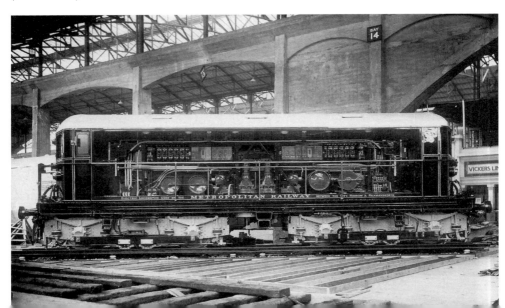

▲ Soon after taking office in 1909, Selbie ordered four more powerful engines to handle the growing freight traffic efficiently. They were supplied by the Yorkshire Engine Co. and designated the G Class, being 0-6-4Ts fitted with Robinson superheaters, and they were delivered in 1915/16. All the engines received names and the above picture shows No.95 *Robert H Selbie* at Neasden Depot. *(R.P. Hendry)*

▼ Another picture of No.95 with an E Class engine at the rather basic Neasden coaling stage. Rather oddly another of the class was named after Charles Jones of the Met – one of the few living chief mechanical engineers to be so honoured. Like most Met engines, their boilers and other components were swapped indiscriminately during overhauls. *(R.P. Hendry)*

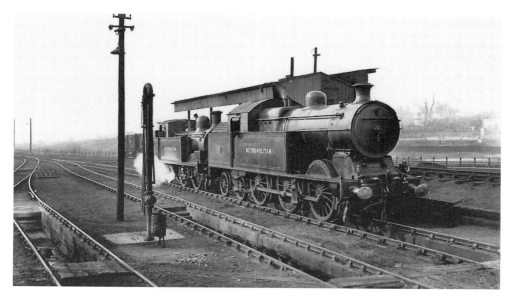

▲ Selbie began planning for the growth in passenger traffic that would arise from his Metroland campaign and wanted a new passenger engine to replace the E Class. Starting in 1920, Kerr Stuart delivered the H Class 4-4-4T engines to a basic design by Neasden. This is a traditional picture by the makers, with No. 106 painted in grey/black to give a good image on the colour-insensitive film of the time. *(Raphael Tuck)*

▼ Here No. 108 drifts through Aylesbury with an up train, displaying the large numbers carried on the bunker of Met engines. The H Class proved to be free-running and their flexible wheelbase allowed them to negotiate sharp curves, such as on the Chesham branch, and soon they came to dominate the Met extension passenger services. They were said to reach 75mph near Chorleywood. *(R. P. Hendry)*

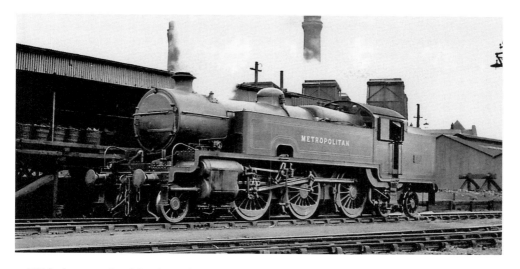

▲ With the growth of freight and the need to minimise its interruption to passenger services, in 1924 Selbie wanted more powerful engines in order to haul longer goods trains. A solution was found in some First World War surplus kits of parts for Maunsell-designed 2-6-0s, made by Woolwich Arsenal. These were assembled for the Met as elegant 2-6-4 tanks by Armstrong Whitworth which could handle loads of up to 600 tons. *(C.A.F. Coll.)*

▼ Another of the powerful K Class engines is here shown at Aylesbury, complete with a Met brake van. As the No.3 Up Goods it had left Verney Junction at 8.10 a.m., shunting at most stations to Rickmansworth and Watford before arriving at Harrow at 9.40 p.m. Selbie had also ensured that the sidings had been lengthened to cope with the extra wagons. *(Robert Clark Coll.)*

▲ Conscious of the drift of passengers to the more luxurious and better-riding coaches of the GCR services, the Met instigated a new design for the steam-hauled trains and this standard was perpetuated with the new multiple-electric T stock. This shows one of the Dreadnought coaches (analogous to the Royal Navy's stately battleships) on an up train at Moor Park. *(Peter Fidczuk Coll.)*

◀ This similar first–class interior of the later T stock shows the great improvement over the previous Ashbury coaches. In later years, when the first–class option had been removed, canny passengers would look out for the wider spacing of the carriage doors in order to be able to relax in the more spacious comfort of an ex–first–class compartment. *(C.A.F. Coll.)*

▲ A serious consequence of Selbie's successful efforts to generate more traffic from the extension was that they created more congestion on the lines south of Harrow into London. Here, at Kilburn High Road in 1915, a new bridge is being erected in order to add a pair of tracks for separate fast and slow running. Nevertheless, in spite of adding extra tracks where feasible, this problem grew. *(Brent Archive)*

▶ In parallel with the track improvements the Met started to restructure Baker Street station. This picture shows works in progress on the other main objective, building a new HQ and complex of flats, shops and a restaurant, reflecting the new-found status of the Met. Firstly the track layout was modified to handle the longer trains, better head shunts and adding a siding to serve the associated flats. *(LTM)*

▲ The platforms were modernised with better access to the Inner Circle and the concourse below for the Bakerloo Line escalators, already carrying 3 million passengers per year by 1911. With the improved track layout and signalling for this crucial junction with the Inner Circle lines, a new signal box was built against the east retaining wall replacing the previous north and junction boxes. *(LTM)*

▼ To power the electrification scheme, in 1904 the Met built its own generating station at Neasden, near the works and staff village – to which it also supplied electricity. This shows the stokers and foremen gathered around one of the steam turbines that drove the generators. Initially the output was some 10.5Mw and this was steadily increased to about 32Mw. *(LTM)*

Met memorabilia. *Top:* A plaque that was mounted in Neasden Works commemorating the chief mechanical engineers, 1863–1933, showing the original and later crests. *Middle:* An engineman's cap badge. *Bottom:* A stationmaster's uniform button, a forty-eight-year-long service medal and a standard uniform button. *(LTM, Brent Archive, C.A.F. Coll.)*

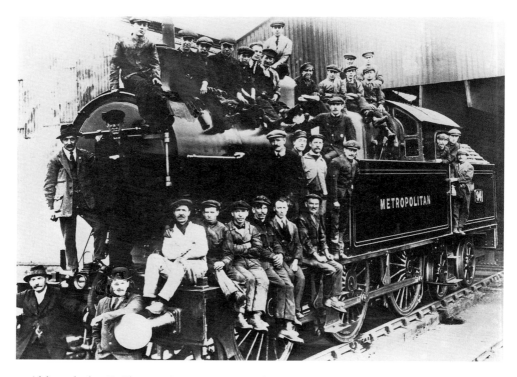

▲ Although the G Class engines were originally intended for the heavier freight trains, the weight of the new Dreadnought coaches brought them into use for passenger traffic. The first of the class, No.94, has here just emerged from an overhaul and repaint at the Neasden Works and seems to be covered by many of the shed staff (and foreman) who obscure its name, *Lord Aberconway*. *(C.A.F. Coll.)*

◄ A group of Met employees in the Neasden paint shop with two of their bowler-hatted foremen on the left. In the background is a newly painted coach of the 1905 Met multiple-electric stock, built by the Metropolitan C&W Co. and finished in the livery of the Hammersmith and City Railway (Met & GW Joint). *(LTM)*

▲ A view from the bridge just north of Neasden station in the late 1920s looking towards Wembley. On the right the tracks lead to the Met Neasden Depot, Works and Power Station, whilst in the centre are their parallel fast and slow lines, and to the far left the LNER tracks from Marylebone which diverge to meet the GW & GCR Joint Line at Northolt. *(Brent Archive)*

▼ A similar view, but from Wembley Park, looking to the south towards Neasden. In the background, the Met Power Station supplies the now predominately electrified tracks. To the left, a set of 1913 electric stock is passing the platform built to serve the Wembley Exhibition, whilst in the centre are two T stock trains and, on the right, an LNER steam train heads for Aylesbury. *(Foxell/Orbit)*

Most railwaymen supported the General Strike called in May 1926 in aid of the coalminers, but only about 20 per cent of the Met and Joint staff went on strike. Selbie was able to run a reduced service with the aid of volunteers and naval stokers to keep the power station working. The strikers returned some ten days later, but over the next few years all staff suffered wage cuts due to the economic situation. The top picture shows the deserted Neasden wheel shop, whilst below a G Class tank became derailed outside Neasden and an attempt is being made by volunteers to re-rail it with the aid of a K Class engine. At the bottom is an armband worn by the Met volunteers. *(Brent Archive)*

▲ Goods were important, generating about a third of the Met's revenue. Coal was the largest item, including the daily coal trains from Stephenson & Clarke which supplied the boilers at Neasden Power Station. There are also a number of their wagons in this train of empties from South Harrow Gas Works emerging from the burrowing junction at Harrow. Note the early LT livery with the interim MET logo. *(C.R.L. Coles)*

▼ Most local coal merchants had their own 'private owners' wagons, often painted in distinctive designs to act as advertising. This example of A.H. Rance, who had a depot in the Chesham yard, had white lettering on a dark-red background. Other well-known coal merchants were Darvell's and Bretnall & Cleland. The goods yards were usually busy with men bagging up and weighing coal for local delivery. *(C.A.F. Coll.)*

▲ Many railways built their goods depots adjacent to the Inner Circle and this was so successful that extra tracks had to be added, called the 'widened lines'. When the Central Meat Market was moved to Smithfield in 1868, the GWR built a depot beneath to access the Met. This shows one of their special 9750 Class 0-6-0 pannier tanks fitted with condensing apparatus to work their trains over the Inner Circle. *(J.J. Smith)*

▼ Met staff were always seeking more business and so when in the First World War a large military camp was opened on the Rothschild Estate at Halton, the nearby Wendover stationmaster persuaded the Met to get the War Office to build a light railway to the camp, using POWs. Until 1963 the Halton Light Railway transported large volumes of supplies to the camp from the Met sidings using their own engines, such as this 0-6-0T. *(C.A.F. Coll.)*

▶ The Chiltern Court flats at Baker Street were served for many years by the Met delivering coal and removing rubbish via a siding off No.1 platform. This is the last of such trains passing Finchley Road in 1961 and it comprised the usual Met Bo–Bo locomotive plus coal wagon A956 and an ex–Met ballast guards van B554. *(LTM)*

▲ Chesham had one of the busiest Met goods yards serving agricultural needs and a wide range of industries including a gasworks, wood and boot factories and a brewery. Typically some 1,700 tons of coal were delivered each year. This shows the yard in front of a standard Met Goods Depot after the absorption by LT in 1933. A Met horse-box van is in the foreground. *(Ray East Coll.)*

▲ Met yards also dealt with special loads such as large boilers, transformers and girders. Here in 1934, a 72 x 6ft girder was brought from Chesham Goods Yard by an LNER tractor lorry to support the circle of the new Embassy Cinema being built in Germain Street. The whole operation was performed at night, as indicated by the town hall clock showing midnight. *(Ray East Coll.)*

▼ The Met made every effort to attract passengers. This shows Robert Geary, a station boy at Chesham, collecting luggage from passengers which would be sent on in advance, ready for their arrival. *(Tony Geary)* Equally, life was made easier when it was possible to buy a ticket from any Met station to anywhere in the UK, via any railway. *(C.A.F. Coll.)*

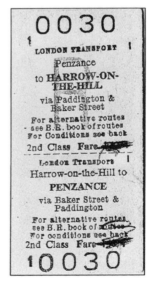

▲ The Met also ran its own extensive parcels service in Metroland and London, as well as distributing newspapers and the Royal Mail. This shows the scene at Aylesbury station where the driver of an ex-Met G Class 0-6-4T No.97 *Brill* watches a postman unloading the mailbags from the luggage compartment of a Dreadnought coach. *(C.A.F. Coll.)*

▼ London Transport (LT) continued the goods and parcels services in conjunction with British Railways (BR) until just after the 1961 electrification of the extension. Before this, the picture of Great Missenden shows the array of barrows awaiting the next delivery via a BR steam-hauled train. *(LTM)* The adjacent stamp for distributing newspapers shows how LT continued the service offered by the Met. *(C.A.F. Coll.)*

▲ A view of Harrow-on-the-Hill station in the 1920s, with Lowlands to the left and the town to the right with the chimney of the Greenhill Laundry. The station had been rebuilt with extra tracks for the Uxbridge branch in 1904 and the substation for the electrification is top right. To the left of Station Road Bridge are the sidings for the changeover from electric to steam traction. *(C.A.F. Coll.)*

▼ The Met had long wanted to build a branch to Watford but this was delayed by the First World War and when preparations started in the 1920s there was considerable disagreement with the LNER over sharing the costs, as the LNER believed that it would mainly benefit the Met. The main contention was over this burrowing junction just north of Harrow to ease the conflict with the Uxbridge trains. *(Met)*

▲ The formal opening of the Watford branch in October 1925 was combined with extending electrification to the new line and Rickmansworth. There was one intermediate station on the branch at Croxley Green, where this first train is passing, with a Bo-Bo electric locomotive hauling a special set of Dreadnought coaches, a Pullman car and the Directors' (ex-Rothschild) Saloon. *(Met)*

▼ The new Watford branch became the responsibility of a Met & LNER sub-committee and optimistically the initial service comprised forty Met and thirty LNER trains each day. However, the General Strike in 1926 gave the LNER the excuse to cancel their trains permanently. Note the characteristic Met 'diamond' logo in deliberate contrast to that of the Underground. *(John Smith)*

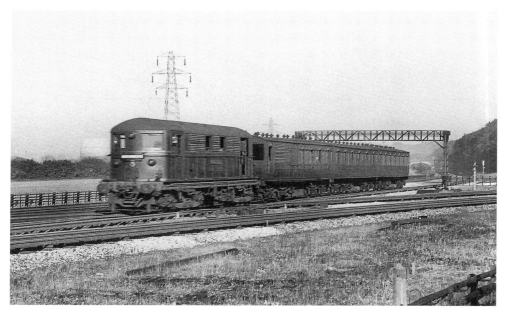

▲ A view looking north with the junction to the new Watford branch to the right. The fast train to London is an MV Bo–Bo electric locomotive No.8, understandably soon to be named *Sherlock Holmes*, hauling a half set of Ashbury bogie coaches. *(L.V. Reason)*

◀ The inside of the junction signal box, located in the middle of the triangular junction near a sub-station. The north curve of the junction had been provided to allow a shuttle service to operate between Rickmansworth and Watford. *(Tony Geary)*

▲ The Met electric train services to Rickmansworth started in 1925 and this now became the changeover point for steam traction. This scene was very familiar to passengers at Rickmansworth waiting during the four-minute changeover: Bo-Bo No.14 *Benjamin Disraeli* has just brought the down train from Aldgate and is running back to take the next train to London. Meanwhile from the primitive coaling siding, a Met H Class No.106 is backing on to take over the down train. *(H.C. Casserley)*

▶ For the changeover, the station man stands astride the centre conductor rail whilst disconnecting the vacuum pipe, as ex-LMS 2-6-4T No.42006 moves forward. Unlikely to be allowed by the Health & Safety Executive! *(F.C. le Manquais)*

▲ A picture of the early Met multiple-electric stock, built in 1905–07 by the Metropolitan Carriage & Wagon Co. to serve the new Uxbridge branch, and here at the then very basic wooden Ickenham station with corrugated-iron shelters and oil lamps. Then in open countryside, the local dairy farmers regularly delivered their milk to the station for delivery to Willesden. *(LTM)*

◀ The previous trains were replaced in the 1920s by the ubiquitous multiple-electric T stock, here in Neasden Depot. The electrical equipment came from Metropolitan-Vickers and there were two basic types, the MV with vacuum brakes and the MW with Westinghouse brakes. The early stock was fully panelled, but later versions were flush-sided using steel sheeting. *(LTM)*

▲ More detail of the T stock is shown in this picture of a train in Northwick Park station. The reason why the gentleman is being ushered into his first-class compartment is because he had come to judge the Met annual station gardens competition. This was an important event and the judges were respected experts. Even the unpromising island platforms, such as this one, were proud of their outstanding flowerbeds. *(LTM)*

▶ Apart from signalling the driver with his green flag, the guard could use the brass-covered handle of his flag to connect two overhead wires which ran the length of many platforms, particularly where there were visibility problems. This action would ring an electric bell at the driver's end of the platform to indicate 'all clear'. *(John Gercken)*

▲ The new Baker Street complex was completed in 1929, designed by the Met architect Charles Clark; it consisted of a HQ, high-class flats and a restaurant built over the station. It was suitably imposing for the growing Met, with a port cochère to provide a covered entrance to the station. This picture shows the contrast with the original entrance to the Met in the foreground at the corner of Baker Street and Marylebone Road. *(C.A.F. Coll.)*

▼ A somewhat earlier picture from the opposite direction, looking at the station surrounded by the flats of Chiltern Court. The signal box on the left, which is soon to be rebuilt, has a Bo-Bo electric locomotive in a bay siding waiting to take out the next train to Rickmansworth. A T stock train for Watford waits in platform 2. *(LTM)*

❖ FIVE ❖

METROLAND

Selbie inherited Watkin's loss-making extension north-west of London, through virtually open country. In order to attract passengers he launched the Metroland project using Watkin's surplus land to create aspirational housing along the Met, so that commuters could benefit from a rural environment and yet easily travel to London. The Metroland campaign created a brand that was propagated using memorable advertising, later immortalised in the works of John Betjeman and others. *(C.A.F. Coll. & Met advertising)*

▲ In many ways, Metroland grew out of Watkin acquiring for the Met the unique ability to redevelop any surplus land. Secondly, when in 1882 he built houses for the staff in the isolated Neasden Works (see above), he realised there was a demand for affordable housing along the extending Met for commuters to London. Thus, the Willesden Park Green Estate was started in 1882 for those of moderate means. *(LTM)*

▼ Selbie developed Met estates out to Amersham, deliberately embracing a range of housing and pricing, and this activity was run by an associated company. These developments formed the core, whilst approved builders created associated estates, such as this one at Barn Hill (near Wembley) by Haymills. In turn, speculative developers tended to add their own housing, riding on the Metroland image. *(C.A.F. Coll.)*

▲ The outstanding example of the use of Watkin's land was the redevelopment of his failed Wembley Pleasure Gardens and Tower. Some of this land was used for the British Empire Exhibition in 1924, here seen in the background to the special platforms created at Wembley Park to cope with the crowds. Furthermore, the remaining 200 acres of land became the Metroland Wembley Park Estate. *(New Zealand Railway Magazine)*

▼ Reid's were typical of the builders encouraged by the Met to create affordable housing near the line from around Harrow out to Uxbridge. Now mortgages had become available such housing was attractive due to its low cost arising from minimal land prices, government subsidies to boost employment, mass-production construction techniques, modern designs and fitments, aggressive marketing and basically the desire for a better life. *(C.A.F. Coll.)*

▲ Another developer of this type was Nash. Here their large hoarding crossed from 411 to 418 in Alexandra Avenue, near Rayners Lane station. Through the triumphal arch the new station can just be seen: a primitive wooden structure, where the passengers were so exposed to the weather that they called it 'pneumonia junction'. By 1930 the number of passengers had grown to about 100,000 p.a. and soon a bustling shopping centre was established around the requisite Odeon Cinema. In 1937 the number of passengers had grown to 4 million p.a. *(C.A.F. Coll.)*

▼ Builders achieved low costs by making large volumes on a production line. This shows how Nash used ex-WD narrow-gauge railways to distribute its materials from the Met sidings. First the roads would be laid to give good access; then the foundations and materials would be bought in large quantities with components like window frames made in their own factory. In this way several houses would be completed each day. *(C.A.F. Coll.)*

▲ As the Met estates were developed further from London, the mix of housing changed from terraced to semi-detached and then detached. The Cedars Estate stretched from Rickmansworth to Chorleywood, comprising mainly detached houses. Here in the morning a commuter to the city, complete with his regulation bowler hat, walks to Chorleywood station beside the Met Estate set in the Hertfordshire countryside. (C.A.F. Coll.)

▼ Not only were the Cedars Estate houses reasonably priced, due to low land costs and the builder's commitment to significant numbers, but the quality of the houses and their surroundings was endorsed by the Metropolitan Railway Country Estates subsidiary of the Met. The brochure illustrates how the introduction of mortgages now made it feasible for people to aspire to their own Metroland home. Selbie himself lived at Chorleywood. (C.A.F. Coll.)

▲ In terms of numbers of houses, most Metroland developments occurred near the Uxbridge branch and this illustrates a typical estate at Ruislip under construction and steadily advancing across the countryside. How long will the oak tree in the foreground survive? However, this virtually mass–production approach meant that you could own such a house for a deposit of £15 and then 10s per week. *(Hillingdon Archive)*

▼ The primitive station at Ruislip Manor opened in 1912, but the First World War delayed housing development and it was not until the 1930s that a new station could be justified. Nevertheless, the goods yard dealt with vast quantities of building materials. In 1933, through the bridge, the work on the associated shopping arcade has been started but it was not until 1938 in the LT era that a new station was opened. *(LTM)*

▲ Lord Ebury, who built the competing LNWR railway from Watford to Rickmansworth, had his stately home at Moor Park. Later this was developed as a golf club and then Lord Leverhulme's property company used it as the focus for building an estate of superior detached houses. It was initially served by a wooden platform station for the benefit of the golf club, called Sandy Lodge. *(C.A.F. Coll.)*

▼ Sandy Lodge station was built (or assembled from odd pieces of wood and corrugated iron) in 1910. A siding was added for local building development but later removed and in 1923 the name became Moor Park & Sandy Lodge. Although the station came to life in 1925 with the opening of the Watford branch giving passengers the option of changing trains here, it remained a classic of Metroland. *(LTM)*

An array of advertising illustrating the range of leisure pursuits the Met felt would be attractive to potential visitors and residents of Metroland. Everything from walking to see the magnificent scenery to traditional hunting, shooting and fishing was available – and why not get there in a luxurious Met Pullman car? *(C.A.F. Coll.)*

▲ Two magnificent coaches were obtained by Selbie from the Pullman Car Co. in 1910, partly to match the GCR and also to attract passengers to Metroland. Business people could have breakfast and then a drink in the evening when returning from the city, whilst wives could lunch in the West End or have a snack on the return from the theatre. Here *Mayflower* is at Aylesbury in 1936. *(H.C. Casserley)*

▼ The Pullmans were specially made to fit the Inner Circle loading gauge, which was 10in narrower than the surface line. They were fitted with Met-type couplings, although these gave trouble over sharp curves. This is the luxurious interior of the other Pullman car *Galatea* (both named after racing yachts) from the bar. Passengers could have a meal for 3*s* and, to go with it, a gin and tonic for 6*d*! *(LTM)*

▲ The Met published an annual 'bible', *Metro-Land*, which combined the attractions of the relevant countryside, the excellent services of the Met for visitors and commuters, and the ready availability of housing for all tastes. Above (left to right) are the striking covers of the first issue in 1916, the 1924 volume marking the British Empire Exhibition, and the final issue in 1932 before the Met was absorbed by LT. *(C.A.F. Coll.)*

▼ The scene at Chalfont & Latimer in the late 1920s, where the Chesham Shuttle has been upgraded to an E Class engine with Dreadnought coaches and the government has re-grouped the mainline railways into four, so that the GCR was now part of the LNER. Bishop Rokeby took this photograph of a group of boys he led on a trip to see the last days of the Met. *(Bishop Rokeby)*

▲ Following the railway grouping in 1923, the government wanted to amalgamate the disparate London train and bus services. The Met fought against this, arguing that it was different to the tube railways, but with Selbie's death in 1930 merger became inevitable. The Met's last defiant act was to open their Stanmore branch in December 1932. Here, in front of the Met 'diamond' logo, are the Met chairman and the Minister for Transport. *(LTM)*

▼ So after seventy years, in January 1933 the Met became part of the new London Transport. This platform garden at deserted Verney Junction was created by a station man who had plenty of spare time. Perhaps it symbolises the sirens that lured Watkin to build his railway out into the wilds of Buckinghamshire in the hope of creating another 'Clapham Junction'? (*H.C. Casserley*)

SIX

FRANK PICK INCORPORATES THE MET INTO LONDON TRANSPORT

The new London Transport of 1933 encompassed virtually all the existing transport activities. The chairman was Lord Ashfield (right) who obtained government backing and financing, whilst Frank Pick as managing director sought to harmonise the disparate companies under a collective, efficient and uplifting brand using the best architects and designers. Even the venerable Met A Class engines soon carried the LT logo. *(LTM)*

▲ Pick obviously regarded the Met as an anomaly in that it combined a high-density inner London service with virtually a steam mainline operation for goods and passengers. Initially some Met locomotives were repainted with 'MET' on their tank sides. Here is No.105, a Class H 4-4-2T, in the yard at Chesham (with the brewery chimney behind) about to take a through train to Rickmansworth for London. *(Real Photographs)*

▼ The first of the H Class tank engines No.103, now in LT service, on 10 December 1937 passing Wendover Dean on a down Aylesbury train. However, earlier in May LT decided to enlarge the Neasden Depot and so arranged with the LNER that they would take over all the ex-Met steam workings beyond Rickmansworth and the relevant locomotives, whilst LT would retain some eleven engines for maintenance work. *(C.A.F. Coll.)*

▲ A very rare picture of an ex-Met K Class engine, No.116, now with London Transport insignia, unusually hauling a passenger train. Usually these handled the heavier goods traffic, but this one leaving Great Missenden heads a down Aylesbury train in November 1937. It had just been transferred to the LNER Depot at Neasden with many of the ex-Met crews, who retained their previous terms and conditions of employment. *(C.A.F. Coll.)*

▼ Soon the ex-Met locomotives were sent to the LNER works at Stratford for some modifications to enable them to operate more widely over the LNER and to repaint them in their livery. Here in 1938 is an H Class 4-4-2T No.94, the last such engine to retain the maroon livery used by the Met. It is just about to leave Great Missenden station with the 8.30 a.m. down train for Aylesbury. *(C.A.F. Coll.)*

▲ The ex-Met K Class engines retained many of their freight duties as shown here in July 1938, where No.116 is shunting a down goods train in Great Missenden station. Note the standard Met water tower in the background. Most of the ex-Met crews who did not transfer with their engines to the LNER 'went on the juice', which was the name for training to become a driver of the Met electric stock. *(C.A.F. Coll.)*

▼ London Transport retained the older E Class tank engines for permanent way and standby duties, as well as the Chesham Shuttle. Here in the winter of 1936 No.1, the original of the class, completes the exhilarating run down into the Chess Valley just before negotiating the reverse bend into Chesham station. Although called the shuttle, at each end of the trip the engine still had to run around the coaches to return. *(C.A.F. Coll.)*

▲ As part of the LT rebuilding of the Met Neasden Depot and Works, it replaced the former primitive engine shed with a smart LT Charles Holden-style building with two tracks. This picture shows an ex-Met E Class locomotive No.77 re-numbered L46 and a Class A tank on display outside their new home. The latter was probably one of those then operating the Brill branch. *(R.P. Hendry)*

▼ Initially, LT maintained the old Met services beyond Aylesbury and this is a classic picture of one such 3.47 p.m. train bound for Verney Junction, pausing in Aylesbury station to take water from the crane and load more parcels. The locomotive is a H Class No.107 4-4-4 tank and the first Dreadnought coach carries the characteristic Verney Junction destination board on its side. Note the original broad-gauge GWR goods shed in the distance. *(H.C. Casserley)*

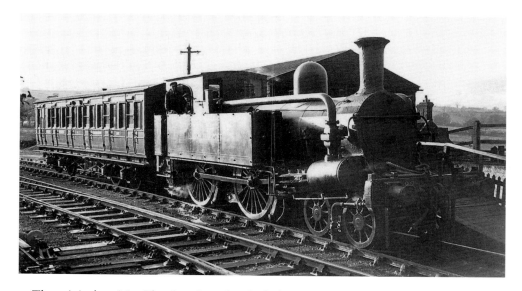

▲ The original ex-Met Class A tank engines had a happy retirement working the light duties of the Brill branch for LT. Here in 1935, No.23 waits for passengers at Brill with its single ex-Met rigid eight-wheeled coach. The few passengers were usually children travelling to school. This duty meant that No.23 survived to take part in the 1963 Met centenary celebrations and is now preserved in the London Transport Museum. *(Robert Clark Coll.)*

▼ Then in July 1935, Pick undertook with the LNER a thorough review of the Joint services beyond Aylesbury and here is the inspection train near Chorleywood, headed by a H Class No.110 with both a Met Pullman and ex-Rothschild Directors' Saloon. The recommendation for closure of the Brill and Verney Junction branches was inevitable in view of the revenues of each being only about £300 p.a. *(LTM)*

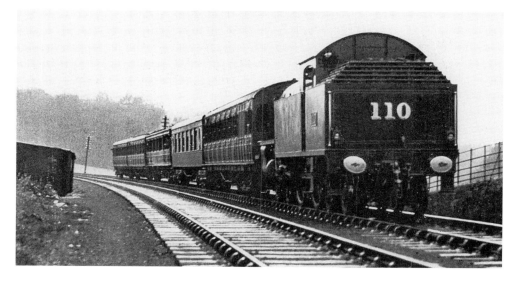

▲ The ex-Met G Class engines became the LNER M2 Class Nos 6154–7 and here, repainted black after an overhaul at their Stratford Works, *Charles Jones* waits in the Rickmansworth coaling siding. They remained at LNER Neasden performing much the same duties on the Met and were scrapped between 1943 and 1948. Some were re-numbered in 1946 as 9075 to 9077 and those that joined British Railways had the prefix 6. *(John Parnham)*

▼ The LNER transferred the ex-Met H Class engines to work in the Nottingham area and replaced them with their own types. However, there was a shortage of locomotives whilst the Met engines they had inherited were being overhauled. This picture shows an ex-GCR Class 9L (now C14) No.6126 4-4-2T, which had longer range than the C13, on loan from Ipswich to help out on the Met. *(Robert Barker)*

Top: Other LNER locomotives began to infiltrate the Joint as they took over operations beyond Aylesbury. Looking north, this shows a train in Aylesbury station with an ex-GER Holden 2-4-2 tank engine No.8307 and auto-coach which has just arrived from Quainton Road. Behind, an ex-GCR Robinson Class J11 0-6-0 tender engine is taking water. These locomotives were nicknamed 'Pom-Poms' because of their characteristic exhaust noise. *(Tony Harden Coll.)*

Middle: By then new LNER-designed engines were also beginning to appear. This traditional 3.20 p.m. down 'Sheffield Special' near Rickmansworth is headed by an ex-GCR Director No.5437 *Prince George* piloting a new Gresley B17 Class 4-6-0. *(Ian Jeayes)*

Bottom: Amongst the LNER tank engines brought in to cover the Met duties were some of the ex-GCR Class B1, now Class L1, powerful 2-6-4Ts nicknamed 'Crabs'. Here No.9067 is working a permanent way train unloading sleepers, just south of Harrow on the LNER tracks. *(C.A.F. Coll.)*

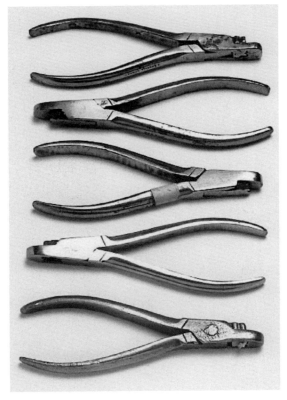

The Met and early LT eras represented the domination of the Edmondson ticketing system. During its reign it was an integral part of railway operations. The passenger having purchased the card ticket, it was examined on entering and leaving the stations and often by an inspector during the journey. Equally, at each stage the ticket would be punched by an identifiable clipper to indicate the route being taken and the validity of the ticket. The tickets would then be sent to the Railway Clearing House to apportion the relevant income to the companies. *(C.A.F. Coll. & LTM)*

▲ Recognising the growth of the Uxbridge branch traffic, under the New Works Programme LT began to upgrade the primitive Met stations to the LT style, covering everything from the architecture, signage and gardens to posters. Harrow-on-the-Hill was the last one to be completed in 1939. This was the imposing College Road entrance, bearing the LT and LNER logos, and with a new signal box towering over it. *(LTM)*

▼ Pick regarded the Met steam services as anomalous to the LT ethos and, as part of their massive New Works Programme funded by the government, he started planning the further electrification of the Met. In the interim, a new GWR diesel railcar No.16 was trialled at Chesham in March 1936. It was only moderately successful and the LT Acton Works were asked to design a more suitable railcar. *(Ray East Coll.)*

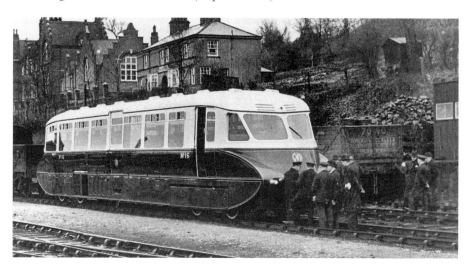

AT LONDON'S SERVICE

LOOKING FOR A HOUSE?
TRY RICKMANSWORTH

In this region of green hillsides and woods, houses and sites are plentiful. To and from Rickmansworth, Chorley Wood, Croxley Green and Moor Park through trains run at short intervals. List of estate agents and builders from

'LONDON TRANSPORT', 55, BROADWAY, S.W.1
VICtoria 6800

See more of the country by living on the
UNDERGROUND

▲ Pick was impressed by the development of Metroland and particularly its contribution to the Met's profits. So at first LT advertising continued the thrust of its predecessor. However, the government regarded this as giving LT an unfair advantage and the relevant Metropolitan housing subsidiary was made a separate company. Thus LT dropped the 'Metroland' brand. *(C.A.F. Coll.)*

▼ By 1938 preparations were under way for the electrification of the Met to Amersham and Chesham. Civil engineering work had started to run four tracks to Rickmansworth and the necessary steelwork for the new bridges was being manufactured. In parallel, Acton Works were busy designing the new multiple-electric rolling stock for the line and this is a mock-up of their first effort in characteristic LT style. *(C.A.F. Coll.)*

▲ The upgrade of the Uxbridge branch was completed with the opening in December 1938 of this new Uxbridge LT station, replacing the original Belmont Road station which became a store for a local tradesman. Designed by Charles Holden, it is similar to the eastern terminus of the Piccadilly Line at Cockfosters. With a striking canopy roof, it has an impressive stained-glass clerestory window at the entrance. *(LTM)*

▼ Whilst many of Pick's actions were regarded as taming the Met, he had more options available for solving the Met's congestion problem at Finchley Road, so he arranged for the Bakerloo Line to be extended to Finchley Road which served the Stanmore branch, thereby alleviating traffic through the Met tunnels to Baker Street. The new Bakerloo Line tracks are in the centre and the scheme was completed just after the outbreak of the Second World War. *(C.A.F. Coll.)*

❖ SEVEN ❖

THE SECOND WORLD WAR

EVACUATION

June 13, 14, 15, 16, 17, 18

On each of the above days certain trains at this station will be reserved for the evacuation of school-children

The trains have been arranged so as to cause the minimum disturbance to ordinary services

LONDON ⊖ TRANSPORT

LT, and therefore the Met, was heavily involved in preparations for the war, from air-raid precautions and manufacturing armaments to evacuating London's children. When the war started the Met was heavily bombed and, although strenuous efforts were made to repair the damage, the lack of maintenance was to hamper post-war services. *(C.A.F. Coll. & LTM)*

▲ In readiness for the war various operational changes were initiated. For example, the moribund Verney Junction branch was reactivated as a diversionary route around London. Even the traditional Chesham branch operation was changed, using an auto–train formation whic h ran as a true 'shuttle', thus avoiding the necessity for the engine to run round the coaches at the end of each journey. Here the 'shuttle' from Chesham passes Raans Farm. (L. V. Reason)

▼ It was ironic that the engines chosen to work this new 'shuttle' were the ex–GCR Class 9K 4-4-2Ts that had worked the early GCR trains to Chesham. This shows one at Chalfont & Latimer, now in LNER livery and numbered 7418, with the 'shuttle' of ex-Ashbury bogie coaches that had been converted to multiple-electric working and then back to steam, before being relegated to the Strategic Reserve. (L. V. Reason)

▲ The whole of the Met territory was bombed throughout the war, but in particular there was the main 1940 Blitz, the 1941 'baby' Blitz and then the V-weapons in 1944–45. This shows the effect of a bomb in November 1940 on Wood Lane station (later White City station) on the Hammersmith & City Line. As many of the surface lines surrounding London were carried on viaducts, such bombs caused severe damage.

▼ An air raid on the night of 29 December 1940 had been particularly devastating, causing major fires in the city. Here is the damage to Aldersgate station (later rebuilt as Barbican station). The upper floors have been gutted and a sign on the frontage advises travellers that there are 'No trains from this Station'. *(LTM)*

▲ On the same night that Moorgate station was hit. As in the earlier picture, this shows the devastated Met Line platforms, with the burnt-out remains of a P-stock train surrounded by the collapsed station canopies.

▼ A further picture of the effect of the air-raid damage at Moorgate, a few days later, when the clear-up was well under way, with a train of ballast wagons filled with rubble, beside a pile of discarded rails. The buildings over the bridge have been completely destroyed. *(LTM)*

▲ In October 1940 a P-stock train was derailed by a bomb near Wembley Park station. Most bomb damage was repaired surprisingly rapidly by manual labour with little assistance from mechanical equipment. Indeed, the resilience of the staff who worked very long hours on meagre rations was quite remarkable.

▼ In May 1941, a bomb fell in the road outside King's Cross station, penetrating the Met line below. This picture clearly shows how with the 'cut and cover' method of construction of the original Met line, the tunnel was only just below the surface of the road. *(LTM)*

Top left: It was during the night of 16 September 1940 that the Kilburn and Brondesbury viaduct bridges were demolished by a high-explosive bomb. Working only during daylight hours, a temporary wooden bridge was built so that the line opened again some thirteen days later.

Top right: Paddington (Praed Street) station was bombed on 14 October 1940, bringing down much debris from the arched roof which killed six people waiting on the platforms for trains. Here the clear-up is in progress with a series of ballast trains removing the rubble.

Bottom: Fortunately the new Met HQ complex at Baker Street was largely of concrete construction on a steel framework, so it withstood to a large extent the air raid of 12 May 1941. Nevertheless, several floors and walls were blown out and here it is possible to look down from the offices above on to platform 1 with a Met train waiting to leave. As mentioned earlier, the Met was able to recover from such attacks surprisingly quickly, but the significant number of UXBs (unexploded bombs) caused longer delays. *(LTM)*

▲ By 1941 the ex-Met H Class 4-4-4T engines transferred to the LNER had been re-allocated to Colwick Shed in Nottinghamshire. Soon the class was fitted with shorter chimneys (ex-GCR), lower domes and cab roofs in order to operate on the local routes. This did not improve their appearance and the new crews did not like these unfamiliar engines. Here ex-No.104 has been renumbered yet again as 7511. (*W.A. Camwell*)

▼ As the war progressed, the Met steam services increasingly relied on ex-GCR locomotives such as the 9K (LNER C13), 9N (LNER A5) and 1B (LNER L1) tank engines, whilst the stalwart Robinson passenger and freight engines continued to dominate the longer-distance Marylebone services. Here, one of the largest of Robinson's express locomotives ex-GCR Class 9P 4-6-0 *Earl Beatty*, now LNER No.6164, pulls out of Aylesbury bound for Marylebone. (*Photomatic*)

❖ EIGHT ❖

NATIONALISATION AND AFTER

During the war the railways had again been placed under the control of the
Railway Executive and so in 1948 the incoming Labour Government nationalised
all transport, with the railways under British Railways. Ironically, the ex-Great
Central Hotel at Marylebone became their headquarters, which, because of their
centralised control and bureaucracy, was nicknamed 'The Kremlin'. Later, in 1963 a
Dr Beeching was to rationalise BR by reducing the number of routes and branches.
(C.A.F. Coll.)

▲ Immediately BR decided to introduce a range of standard locomotives and, in order to find the best features of existing engines, some trials were conducted over the Joint Line. Here, the ex–Southern Railway mixed–traffic choice of West Country No. 34006 *Bude* enters Marylebone in June 1948 with the LNER dynamometer car behind. However, the trials were inconclusive. Note the IMS milk depot in the background, which received regular shipments over the Joint. *(B.W.L. Brooksbank)*

▼ BR was soon sub-divided into regions and so the old sharing of the Joint continued under LT initially with the Eastern Region of BR but, after the war, track and engines were in a bad state of repair and the ex-Met locomotives of LT were often called upon to haul the scheduled services. LT No. 46 (ex-Met No. 77) is in the bay platform at Aylesbury station, about to take out the 8.30 a.m. to Baker Street. *(C.A.F. Coll.)*

▲ Another instance when, due to shortages, a scheduled engine had been replaced by one that happened to be available. One of the Chesham branch locomotives, LNER No.7418 Class C13 4-4-2T is leaving Moor Park & Sandy Lodge station with the Saturdays–only 1.41 p.m. Wendover to Marylebone train on 27 September 1947. *(Millbrook House)*

▼ The remaining ex-Met locomotives retained by LT still remained busy with their ongoing role as standby engines, maintenance and permanent way work, and local movement of goods trains. This picture shows one of the Peckett saddle tanks ex-Met No.102 and now LT No.L53 passing through Willesden Green station with a train of coal wagons in 1956. *(Fred Ivey / David Bosher)*

▲ In 1956, LT No.46 was again allocated to standby duties at Aylesbury and it is in the bay platform taking water. A train for Marylebone is on the other side of the platform but the attention of the schoolboys is concentrated on the ex-Met tank engine. The interest of boys was at its peak, boosted by the post-war publication by Ian Allan of his popular ABC books, listing for the first time the numbers and details of all the engines. *(Robert Clark Coll.)*

▼ In 1959, coal still remained the dominant fuel for heating, and LT continued to handle substantial traffic over the Joint and Met Lines. L52, the ex-Met F Class 0-6-2T No.93, is shown here shunting such coal wagons at Willesden Green sidings. However, the ex-Met engines were becoming uneconomical to overhaul and consideration was given by LT to obtaining diesel replacements. In 1962 L52 was the penultimate Met engine to be withdrawn. *(Fred Ivey/David Bosher)*

▲ North of Moor Park station, where the Met crosses over the Grand Union Canal, gravel pits were excavated with sidings to remove it for the construction of Watkin's railways. That area became part of the junction for the new Watford branch, but the gravel pits became Met/LT waste dumps. This shows an LT train heading for The Tip, hauled by L52, having reversed at Watford, and using the South Curve to access the sidings. *(L.V. Reason)*

▼ The other surviving ex-Met F Class No.L50 is seen here in 1956, a year before being withdrawn, on a down breakdown train including the LT Ransome & Rapier crane. It is en route for Amersham and is passing the little-used North Curve at the junction for the Watford branch. Originally this curve was for a shuttle service between Rickmansworth and Watford. Operated by a single T stock unit, it was withdrawn due to bus competition. *(S. Gradidge Coll.)*

▲ The ex-Met locomotives were now being withdrawn for scrapping and here L44, the first of the Met E Class 0-4-4 tank engines, awaits its fate in Bedfordshire. Fortunately recognising its significance, the London Railway Preservation Society saved the engine and eventually moved it to the Buckinghamshire Railway Centre at Quainton, where it was later restored to working order as Met 1. Subsequently it has taken part in many special events. *(C.A.F. Coll.)*

▼ Some of the ex-Met MV Bo-Bo electric locomotives were deemed not worth repairing and had been scrapped for spares. Then, with the extension beyond Rickmansworth being electrified in 1961, the result was that only four were kept for shunting duties. This shows No. 1 *John Lyon* at Neasden, after a fractured bogie truck had been found which was uneconomical to repair, and then it too was eventually scrapped for spares in 1972. *(C.A.F. Coll.)*

▲ Having rejected diesel traction, LT chose the ex-BR/GWR 57xx Class 0-6-0 pannier tanks as suitable replacements for their ageing Met engines and eventually bought thirteen of them between 1956 and 1963. They were suitably modified with trip-cocks to operate the signalling over electrified tracks and one of their regular turns was to haul the trains of LT waste to the Croxley Junction Tip for disposal. (S. Gradidge Coll.)

▼ Another ex-GWR pannier tank locomotive No.L90 passing through Wembley Park station with empty permanent way low-loading wagons in 1959. When repainted by LT these locomotives looked very smart in their maroon finish with yellow lining. However, even these engines were reaching the end of their useful lives and repairs became more difficult. (David Bosher)

▲ The ex-GWR pannier tanks also took over the breakdown turns with the LT Ransome & Rapier crane, as shown here at Rickmansworth. But their reign came to a fitting conclusion when in 1971, to mark the end of 100 years of steam haulage on the Met, LT held a 'Farewell to Steam' event. Then a pristine maroon pannier, No.L94 took a train from Moorgate through the original Met tunnels to Neasden for the last time. *(Fred Ivey/David Bosher)*

▼ Taken from the long lattice footbridge just south of Rickmansworth station, the ex-GWR pannier tank locomotive passes underneath in a cloud of exhaust with an ex-Met Dreadnought third/brake coach bound for repair at Neasden. To the right is a set of T stock awaiting return to Baker Street. It was ironic that the GWR provided the engines for the beginning and end of Met scheduled steam services. *(Fred Ivey/David Bosher)*

▲ In the post-war years the LT P stock dominated the Met Uxbridge branch services and here, in 1952, a typical example in red LT livery passes Dollis Hill station island platform with a fast Baker Street train. Originally the P stock was fitted with the new Metadyne control equipment but this was found to be unreliable and was replaced by PCM gear. *(Fred Ivey/ David Bosher)*

▼ By the mid-1950s the new standard designs of BR locomotives were beginning to replace the pre-war engines. Again from the footbridge at Rickmansworth, such a new BR 2-6-0 tender locomotive Class 4 No.76039 shunts the daily pick-up goods train in the goods yard. In the background, in the goods shed bay, is ex-Met Bo-Bo No.13 *Dick Whittington*, still in its wartime plain grey livery. *(Fred Ivey/David Bosher)*

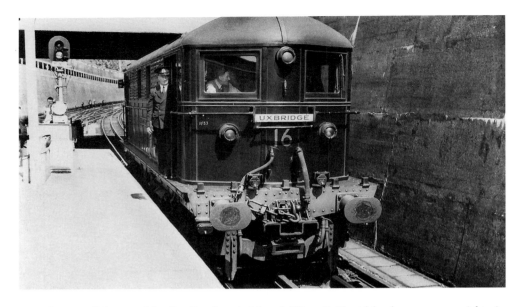

▲ In fine condition, ex–Met Bo–Bo electric No. 16 *Oliver Goldsmith* backs on to a special train at Uxbridge station in 1954. Later, on 9 September 1961, it took part in the official farewell run to Amersham using steam locomotives, but on return to Neasden that night it was placed in a siding ready for scrapping. However, it was first used for tests by BR at Willesden before being cut up at Rugby in 1966. *(Fred Ivey/David Bosher)*

▼ A picture that captures the isolation and primitive nature of Moor Park & Sandy Lodge station in 1954. The T stock train is somewhat confusingly carrying destination boards to both Rickmansworth and Watford. The majority of the passengers using the platforms were either children from the local schools or those changing trains between the mainline and the Watford branch. In 1958 the station was to be renamed Moor Park. *(Fred Ivey/David Bosher)*

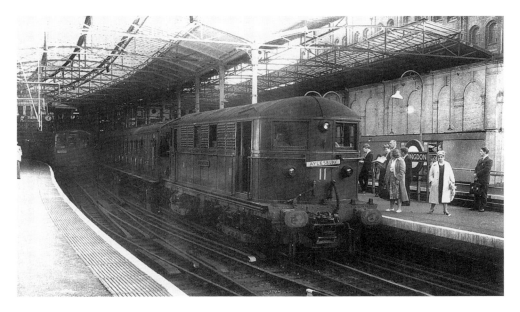

▲ Ex-Met Bo-Bo electric locomotive No.11 *George Romney* awaits departure at Farringdon with a train of Dreadnought coaches bound for Aylesbury in 1954. To the right are the widened lines and the station awnings are replacements for those destroyed by the wartime bombing. *(Fred Ivey/David Bosher)*

▼ LT F stock on the ex-Met East London Line at Whitechapel station in 1957. Originally the station logo would have been of the Met diamond design, but in green to signify the East London Line. *(Fred Ivey/David Bosher)*

▲ The scene at the throat of Liverpool Street station in 1961. Ex-Met Bo-Bo electric locomotive No.16 *Oliver Goldsmith* is in the refuge siding on the left, waiting to back on to the next train. On the right an LT COP stock Metropolitan Line train emerges from the tunnel bound for Barking. *(Fred Ivey/David Bosher)*

▼ Another picture from the Rickmansworth footbridge, overlooking the goods yard busy with coal merchants. Beside the cattle dock bay are an array of ex-Met Bo-Bo electrics (No.2 *Thomas Lord*, ex–*Oliver Cromwell*, No.4 *Lord Byron* and No.18 *John Wycliffe*) waiting their turn to take the next trains back to London. Meanwhile, an ex-LMS BR 2-6-4T designed by Fairburn in 1945 arrives with a train from Marylebone. *(Fred Ivey/David Bosher)*

▲ A post-war picture of Moorgate station looking eastwards with most of the bomb-damaged buildings demolished but before the major redevelopment got under way. On the left is an LT F stock train with an ex-Met T stock set beside it. On the widened lines is an ex-LNER Gresley Class N2/2 condensing 0-6-2 tank engine, built with a short chimney in order to comply with the Met loading gauge. (C.A.F. Coll.)

▼ In 1952 LT remained pessimistic about funding to further electrify the extension, and again an attempt was made to replace the anachronistic Chesham Shuttle, so a three-car set of ACV lightweight 125hp diesel rail buses were borrowed for trials. These ran for two weeks in October, as pictured here at Chalfont & Latimer, with a trusty C13 as backup. The rail buses struggled with the sharp bends and could not handle wagons. (Ron White)

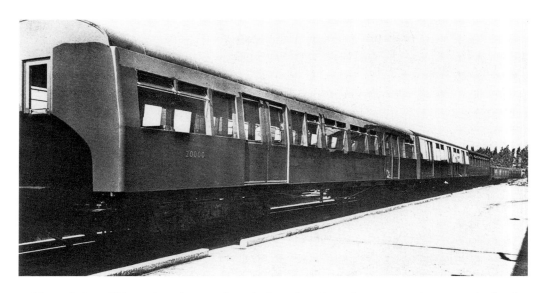

▲ Nevertheless, LT continued to explore designs, based on the pre-war Acton work, for the multiple-electric stock that would be needed for the possible electrification scheme. After experimenting with several mock-ups, two trial cars with different seating arrangements were built (Nos 17000 and 20000), using T stock under-frames salvaged from damaged coaches. Both were fitted with sliding doors and a guard's position to control them. *(C.A.F. Coll.)*

▼ For safety considerations in tunnels both coaches had sliding doors and through gangways. The interior of No.17000 (right) in fact had gangways on one side with four abreast seating, whilst No.20000 had a central gangway with two abreast seats on either side. Both were fitted with the traditional Met luggage and umbrella racks. In practice the layout of No.20000 was favoured but further modified for the final design. *(C.A.F. Coll.)*

▲ Surprisingly, in view of the small capital budgets for railways at that time, in 1956 LT was given the £3.5 million to complete the Met electrification programme. A lot of the civil engineering work had been finished before the war and 'mothballed', as can be seen in this picture of ex-Met Bo-Bo electric No.1 *John Lyon* with a Chesham train near Pinner, showing ground prepared on the right for the extra fast tracks. *(Fred Ivey/David Bosher)*

▼ In spite of the preparations, in 1961 much needed to be done, like the major widening of the Northwood bridge. Fairfield's of Chepstow had delivered the extra girders before the war and they were stored on site. Here the work is recommencing on the new slow tracks, with a train hauled by Bo-Bo No.8 *Sherlock Holmes* crossing the existing span and appropriately destined for Baker Street. *(LTM)*

▲ Initial trials of the electrification to Amersham and Chesham were performed with the venerable T stock trains which revealed only a few problems with the power-feeding arrangements. This picture shows such a T stock train in Amersham station, looking south, with a down Aylesbury-bound train in the far platform. At that time steam power still took over at Rickmansworth for the service beyond Amersham. *(R. P. Hendry Coll.)*

▼ Another trial train in early 1961, this time a set of LT red COP stock arriving at Amersham station. The station had been remodelled with two extra tracks on the right to deal with the Marylebone services. In addition a new signal box was built further to the right of this picture, which controlled a much longer section from Rickmansworth, including the Chesham branch. *(Fred Ivey/David Bosher)*

▲ The end of steam power over the Met was in sight and its remaining classic example was the Chesham Shuttle. Although the original Met engines had been replaced by the C13s and then a succession of BR tank engines, as in the above picture of BR Ivatt 2-6-2T No.41272 crossing one of the bridges over the River Chess, the train with its venerable Ashbury coaches was a memorable vision. *(Fred Ivey/David Bosher)*

▼ Finally the Chesham branch was electrified, including a new bay platform, which in theory would enable more trains to run over the branch. The last steam service ran on 11 September 1960 and here another BR Ivatt tank engine No.41287 is decorated with the traditional laurel wreath on the smokebox door, whilst the driver poses for the occasion during the day. *(Tony Harden Coll.)*

▲ The inaugural electric train leaving Chesham on 12 September 1960. It comprised a stalwart T stock four-car set as there were delays in the delivery of enough of the new A60 units. For this important occasion the town mayor, Dr Arnold Baines, was riding in the cab, having also travelled on the special last steam Chesham Shuttle, hauled by the restored ex-Met 1, at midnight the day before. *(C.A.F. Coll.)*

▼ On 9 September 1961 LT ran a special train marking the end of their steam-hauled services beyond Rickmansworth and here in Amersham station BR No.42070 ex-LMS Fairburn 2-6-4 T waits to go back to Rickmansworth. In recent times these engines had been provided by the London Midland Region of BR, which was replacing its own commuter trains by diesel multiple units and deliberately running down its longer-distance services from Marylebone. *(CAF Coll.)*

▲ With car No. 5009 in the foreground, one of the first A60 stock to be delivered is on an up train at Northwood station in 1961. The new cars had lightweight aluminium bodies on steel under-frames and all the axles of the end cars in a four-car set were motorised. Behind is the original Met signal box, soon to be phased out, whilst in the background the land has been cleared for the extra two tracks, which at this point became the slow lines. *(Fred Ivey/ David Bosher)*

▼ The new A60 stock encounters the Chiltern winter at Chesham for the first time early in the morning in January 1962, after the branch was blocked by heavy snow for three days. Note that the snow has been cleared from the unused new bay platform and the station man still has to unload parcels for local delivery. Also the ex-GWR water tower remains in the background. *(C.A.F. Coll.)*

▲ During their service the LT A60 stock received two major upgrades at the ADtranz Derby Works. Apart from general refurbishment, the opportunity was taken to make significant changes. The A60 sets were taken to Derby via the Joint Line by ex-BR Class 37 diesels using a buffer wagon to match the different couplings. This shows such a train leaving Neasden Depot in 1997 for Derby, hauled by EW&S 35057 *Viking. (Kim Rennie/ LURS)*

▼ In the 1997 upgrade the opportunity was taken to remove the guard's position as that role had been abolished. This picture recalls the presence of such guards, with 'Ernie' Woodstock the then stationmaster of Chalfont & Latimer – who had risen from being a pre-war station boy – talking to one of the guards. A later upgrade resulted in windows being added at the ends of the coaches to improve security. *(C.A.F. Coll.)*

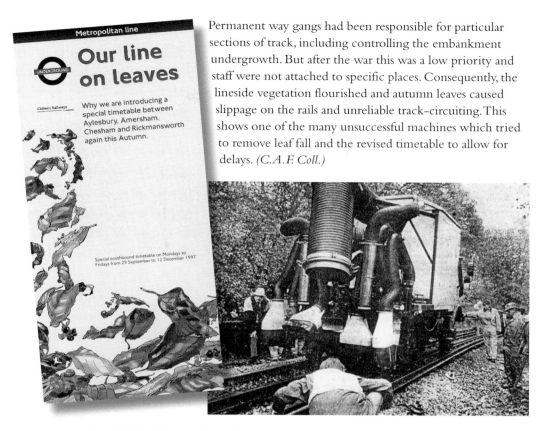

Metropolitan line

Our line on leaves

Chiltern Railways — Why we are introducing a special timetable between Aylesbury, Amersham, Chesham and Rickmansworth again this Autumn.

Special southbound timetable on Mondays to Fridays from 29 September to 12 December 1997

Permanent way gangs had been responsible for particular sections of track, including controlling the embankment undergrowth. But after the war this was a low priority and staff were not attached to specific places. Consequently, the lineside vegetation flourished and autumn leaves caused slippage on the rails and unreliable track–circuiting. This shows one of the many unsuccessful machines which tried to remove leaf fall and the revised timetable to allow for delays. *(C.A.F. Coll.)*

Due to lack of funds to replace the weakened original Met bridges over the River Chess, LT wanted to terminate the Chesham branch at the moor on the outskirts of the town. This is where Watkin had originally intended to build the station. Fortunately at the eleventh hour support came from Ken Livingstone via the GLC Residuary Body. Here in March 1986 the new span is about to be slid across to replace the former two bridges at the moor. *(Clive Foxell Coll.)*

▲ Because of the disparate interests in the Joint, BR kept changing which of their regions had responsibility. Initially, on nationalisation Eastern Region inherited the previous LNER operations with rolling stock that had been worked hard during the war and poorly maintained. Many of these were ex-GCR engines as shown in this picture of a Robinson shapely Atlantic, dubbed *Jersey Lilies* after the Edwardian singer Lily Langtry, passing through desolate Moor Park & Sandy Lodge in 1948. *(H.C. Casserley)*

▼ Gradually, Eastern Region tried to restore their run-down services and more Gresley locomotives started to reappear. Typical were the V2 Class of 2-6-2s and here in January 1955, amid an overnight fall of snow and having left Marylebone for Aylesbury, No.60815 is working hard climbing the Chilterns towards Dutchlands summit with the regulator well open at about 50–55mph. *(D.A. Dant)*

▲ The flagships of this effort were the named expresses, *The South Yorkshireman* and here in 1958, the other express, an up *The Master Cutler* just past Chorleywood station headed by Gresley Class A3 No.60111 *Enterprise*. But control soon passed to London Midland Region, marking a run-down of services due to their view that these represented competition with their own trains based at St Pancras. In addition, there was the move to BR locomotives, then the decline of steam power. *(S. Gradidge Coll.)*

▼ In 1962, Midland Region was forced to use Marylebone more due to the redevelopment of Euston. Consequently this up excursion has been diverted over the Joint through Rickmansworth. The train is headed by BR Britannia Class 4-6-2 No.70048 *The Territorial Army 1908–1958*, then based at Neasden. One of the new standard BR range built in 1954, the impending switch to diesel locomotives meant that it was scrapped in 1967. *(S. Gradidge Coll.)*

▲ Most of the Met Line route over the Chilterns was over 400ft above sea level and subject to frequent snow in winter. Here on a snowy New Year's Day in 1962, a brand-new south-bound A60 multiple-electric stock train pauses at Rickmansworth beside the (still in use) water crane. In the bay platform is an ex-CLR electric car converted for de-icing duties over the Met. *(LTM)*

▼ The Marylebone commuter services were now in the hands of the ubiquitous diesel multiple units and, following the reversal of the decision to close Marylebone, their popularity significantly increased passenger numbers. This view of Wendover station shows a typical BR Derby-built DMU eight-car set passing the yard which gave access to the Halton Light Railway serving the RAF camp. On the left is a preserved Met signal box . *(Tony Harden Coll.)*

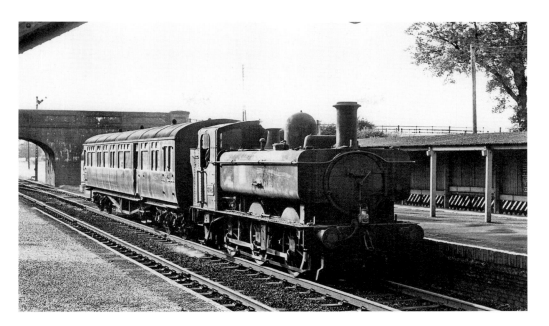

▲ Another steam service over the old Joint beyond Aylesbury was a shuttle train from the Western Region at Princes Risborough to Quainton Road. Here an ex-GWR Class 54xx 0-6-0 pannier tank engine is bringing its autocar trailer back into Quainton Road station for the return journey. The passenger service here was withdrawn in 1963 and the goods facilities in 1966. *(Dr G. C. Farnell)*

▼ The English Electric experimental 4-6-0 locomotive No.GT3. A 2,700hp gas turbine mechanically powered a conventionally outlined locomotive on Class 5 frames, with the diesel fuel carried in the tender. The under-used Joint Line was an ideal route for the BR trials, seen here at Rickmansworth in 1961, but in spite of encouraging performance, it was scrapped in 1966 in view of the BR 'push to diesel'. *(Fred Ivey/David Bosher)*

▲ Another stranger to the Joint in the last days of steam was this ex-Ministry of Supply Austerity 2-8-0, purchased by BR in 1948. They were designed by Riddles during the war and he incorporated some of the features in his later BR standard locomotive designs. Here No.90520 is seen plodding out of Wendover with long goods bound for Willesden. *(L.V. Reason)*

▼ Finally, the last scheduled steam train over the Joint ran on 3 September 1966. Packed with enthusiasts, it was a Marylebone to Nottingham train hauled by a typical grimy BR Class 5 4-6-0 No.45292, with the forlorn message 'THE LAST DAY – GREAT CENTRAL' chalked on the smokebox door. The train is leaving Harrow-on-the-Hill station to pass under a Roxborough Road bridge lined with spectators. *(B.H. Jackson)*

▸ However, there was a resurgence of steam over the Met when, in 1989, a number of local people felt that the centenary of the opening of the Chesham branch in 1889 should be properly celebrated. This led to the town council, local businesses and like-minded LT managers organising a week of special events centred on a train 'topped & tailed' by the restored Met 1 and preserved Bo–Bo *Sarah Siddons*. *(Clive Foxell Coll.)*

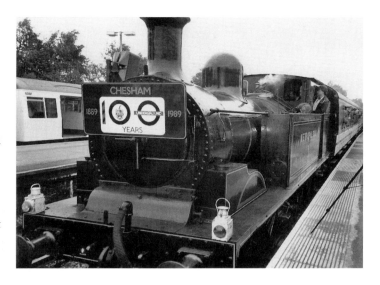

▾ This centenary celebration inaugurated a popular annual 'Steam on the Met' event, running between Amersham, Watford and Harrow. This picture shows when, in 1999, the special train was headed by a preserved BR Class KI 2-6-0 No.62005 of LNER origins, supported by a Class 22 diesel locomotive. Sadly, more stringent health and safety regulations, coupled with a less enthusiastic management culture, brought these events to an end the next year. *(Clive Foxell Coll.)*

▲ The undoubted highlight of the later 'Steam on the Met' events was the spectacular parallel running of two steam trains over the LT four-track section. Making an impressive start from Harrow in 1996 were two ex-GWR preserved engines, on the right pannier No.9466, which would run over the fast tracks to Amersham, and on the left Mogul No.7325, which would diverge after Moor Park to go on to Watford. *(Ron Potter)*

▼ Representing the state of the Joint by the end of the last millennium. In the foreground at Chalfont & Latimer station is a refurbished A60 four-car set with the Chesham Shuttle. Behind it is an Aylesbury-bound Turbo165 DMU of Chiltern Railways, the privatised operating company which had taken over all the Marylebone services and under Adrian Shooter had become one of the best performers in the UK. *(Clive Foxell Coll.)*

❖ NINE ❖

INTO THE TWENTY-FIRST CENTURY

These pictures represent the major changes happening to the Met. Firstly, after some fifty years of staunch service, the LT A60 stock are being replaced by new trains and a significant consequence was the end of the Chesham Shuttle after some 116 years. Here in the cab of the celebratory last shuttle are driver Paul Hawkins and the author, who gave a commentary during the trip. Secondly the future, with a view of the interior of the new LT S stock (S for sub-surface), which are replacing all the LT A, C and D stocks. *(Clive Foxell Coll.)*

◀ In 2003 the Met became part of Metronet, a private consortium formed under a controversial Government Private Finance Initiative, upgrading the Transport *for* London sub-surface lines. This shows Amersham track replacement under way using a leased GBRf Class 66 diesel, carrying the ex-GCR nameplate *Valour*, previously on their First World War remembrance engine. By 2008, with timescales slipping and costs rising, the contracts were returned to T*f*L. *(Clive Foxell Coll.)*

▼ As deliveries of their replacements have started, the end is nigh! A fine 2011 picture of an A60 stock train in the latest LT livery on the Uxbridge branch at Ruislip. It is beside an externally well-preserved ex-Met signal box. The A60s were made up of four-car sets with the end cars having powered axles. Capable of 70mph, they were usually limited to 60mph. *(Paul Green)*

▲ The replacements for the LT A60 stock were ordered from Bombardier during the Metronet period. Based on their Movia design, all axles are powered giving greater acceleration, but the top speed has been restricted to 60mph. The first of the production was delivered in February 2009 and this picture shows a GBRf Class 66 diesel locomotive No.66729 bringing an S stock set from the Bombardier test site at Old Dalby. *(Gareth Bayer)*

▼ The S stock for the Met Line, being in an eight-car set, is incompatible with the shorter Chesham Shuttle formation, so after 116 years of service it has been replaced by the eight-car set running as a through service to London – much to the pleasure of Chesham commuters. The last day of shuttle operation was 11 December 2010 and the Met management made it an occasion by running a celebratory train with commemorative tickets. *(Clive Foxell Coll.)*

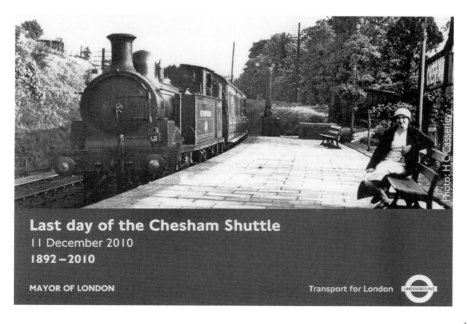

Last day of the Chesham Shuttle
11 December 2010
1892–2010

MAYOR OF LONDON   Transport for London UNDERGROUND

▲ The celebratory last shuttle arriving at Chesham station at midday. Being such a part of the life of the town, it was packed with local people as well as enthusiasts. One special headboard was raffled for charity and the other given to Chesham Museum. The actual last shuttle ran at midnight and returned to Neasden Depot. Then eight-car A60 stock took over the new service whilst deliveries of the new S stock arrived. *(Clive Foxell Coll.)*

▼ A new S stock train in service between Watford and Baker Street: an S8 (eight-car) variant for the Met with a higher proportion of seating to standing as compared with S7 (seven-car) sets for the other sub-surface inner London lines. Even so there is a 30 per cent reduction in seating compared with the previous A60 stock. Many station platforms, including Baker Street, have been lengthened to accommodate the longer coaches in the S8 formation. *(Paul Green)*

▶ The design of the S stock has many features to improve passenger use. They are air conditioned, coaches are interconnected – all with CCTV – floors should be level with the platform for wheelchair access and displays will provide much more information. It is expected that all the 191 new S stock trains will be delivered by 2013 and A stock phased out on the Met during 2012. *(Clive Foxell Coll.)*

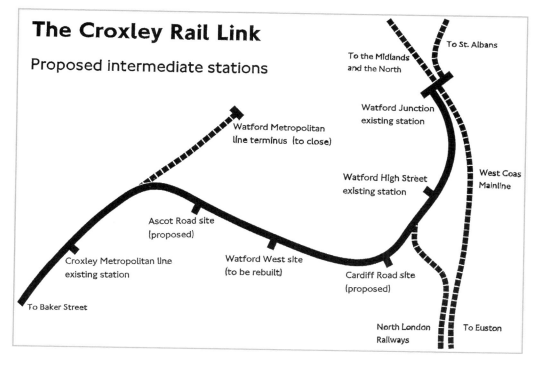

The Croxley Rail Link

Proposed intermediate stations

To the Midlands and the North

To St. Albans

Watford Junction existing station

Watford Metropolitan line terminus (to close)

Watford High Street existing station

West Coast Mainline

Ascot Road site (proposed)

Croxley Metropolitan line existing station

Watford West site (to be rebuilt)

Cardiff Road site (proposed)

To Baker Street

North London Railways

To Euston

▲ After the new trains, does the Met have any fresh fields to conquer? Well, it would seem that the success of Chiltern Railways will preclude any recovery of Watkin's far-flung empire when the Oxford–Verney Junction–Bedford line is reinstated. But the possibility of achieving the Met's ambition to get to the centre of Watford has been kept alive by a popular proposal to join the Met at Croxley Green to the nearby moribund ex-LMS branch into the centre of Watford. *(Clive Foxell Coll.)*

If you enjoyed this book, you may also be interested in…

The Metropolitan Line: London's First Underground Railway
CLIVE FOXELL

This is the fascinating history of the world's first underground passenger railway, built in 1863 to ease the traffic congestion of a growing London and thus creating the first metro system. Featuring many previously unpublished photographs, it is a must for all railway enthusiasts and social historians.

978-0-7524-5396-5

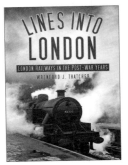

Lines Into London: London Railways in the Post-War Years
WRENFORD J. THATCHER

This collection of evocative photographs is divided into eastern, southern, western and midland regions, revealing the changes occurring on the London railways in the post-war years. From Euston and Paddington out to the suburbs all around London and the wider UK, these stunning, previously unpublished images beautifully record the mood of the late '40s, '50s and '60s, and the last great days of steam.

978-0-7524-5892-2

London's Great Railway Century 1850–1950
KEITH SCHOLEY

This fascinating book explores the many contemporary transport themes of London's termini, including goods depots, electrified lines, industrial railways and Southern suburban lines. Covering the pivotal century from 1850–1950, each chapter describes a decade and an issue particularly relevant to that period. With fresh research, there are gems to delight commuter, resident and tourist alike.

978-0-7524-6291-2

The Chiltern Railways Story
HUGH JONES

The story of the most successful of Britain's new private railway companies is one of triumphant business despite the odds. Formed in 1996 after the privatisation of British Rail, this is a modern railway history, and one which reveals the secrets behind running a good public transport service. Incorporating previously unpublished images from the Chiltern archives, this book looks at significant events in the company's history.

978-0-7524-5454-2

Visit our website and discover thousands of other History Press books.

www.thehistorypress.co.uk

The History Press